Behind the Scenes of Health Care

Behind the Scenes of Health Care

Motivation and Commitment of Health Care Employees

Dr. Hesston L. Johnson

BEP BUSINESS EXPERT PRESS

First published in 2020 by
Business Expert Press, LLC
222 East 46th Street, New York, NY 10017
www.businessexpertpress.com

ISBN-13: 978-1-95152-738-9 (paperback)
ISBN-13: 978-1-95152-739-6 (e-book)

Business Expert Press Health Care Management Collection

Collection ISSN: 2333-8601 (print)
Collection ISSN: 2333-861X (electronic)

Cover and interior design by S4Carlisle Publishing Services Private Ltd., Chennai, India

First edition: 2020

10 9 8 7 6 5 4 3 2 1

Printed in the United States of America.

Abstract

Behind the Scenes of Health Care presents an extensive review of motivation and commitment among health care workers in support and bedside care roles. The publication includes two research studies: (1) motivation and commitment of support services employees in a health care environment and (2) the correlation between patient experience feedback and nursing motivation and engagement. Additionally, the publication includes two case studies: (1) cultural disruption in a health care system and (2) a service organization review of turnover. Lastly, and most significantly, the publication provides a framework and model, *The Tri-Factor Model*, to assess and measure workplace dynamics of motivation, commitment, and culture that is also applicable to turnover analyses. Readers of *Behind the Scenes of Health Care* are provided tools to understand motivation, commitment, and cultural components in the contemporary workplace that may be applied to any organization.

Keywords

health care leadership; organizational commitment; workplace motivation; motivation factors; patient experience; patient feedback; nursing engagement; health care service workers; support service employees; affective organizational commitment; continuance organizational commitment

Contents

Preface

The study of motivation, commitment, and culture can lead to pragmatic and logical assumptions. However, leaders' comprehension in terms of costs, organizational performance, and cultural development are factors inhibited by poorly developed environments. There often is an unbalanced perception of what motivates employees to a level of commitment and how to develop culture. As such, I have tackled current research and seminal observations to develop models and describe outcomes associated with each construct. This book includes two health care employee studies: motivation and commitment among service workers, and the relationships between employee engagement and patient experience feedback. Additionally, this book includes two case studies: workforce turnover in a services organization, and cultural disruption in a health care system. Lastly, this book includes a theoretical model for assessment, understanding, and action related to workplace motivation, commitment, and organizational culture.

The components of this book were crafted over roughly 4 years to include case studies, dissertation proposals, and professional observations. Much of the selection and editing of the manuscript took place while on a personal hiatus to Alaska to celebrate the completion of my doctoral degree. In a strange way, perhaps, I find writing to be a soothing activity and the thought of completing my second book exhilarating. When coupling the enjoyment with a backdrop of the majestic mountain ranges of Alaska, magic can happen during the most frustrating times of the writing process.

All of that aside, thank you for holding my book in your hands and taking the time to explore my love for organizational behavior, workplace motivation, and organizational commitment. This book is written for many people, including managers, executive leaders, academics, and general practitioners. However, it is a book written mostly for myself and for those like myself, experiencing and observing the interactions of workplace culture, employee motivations, and professional career components of identifying how and why people behave as they do and why they stay with their employers.

I truly hope you enjoy this multifaceted journey of experience and observations as much as I have enjoyed putting it together. All research clearances were provided by those involved. NIH certification and HIPAA for Researchers was obtained prior to the research conducted within this book.

With my greatest gratitude,
Dr. Hesston L. Johnson

CHAPTER 1

Culture and Employment

The time an individual stays with his or her employer is increasingly becoming more about elements of organizational culture, motivation, and outcomes driving individual organizational commitment. Organizational culture is composed of norms within an organization that impresses upon employees workplace experiences, expectations, organizational philosophy, and acceptable behaviors. Culture is also composed of shared beliefs, attitudes, and relationships indicating expected group behaviors.

When considering culture, motivation, and turnover, the phenomenon of an endless existence of turnover challenges has, as of late, been further complicated by the improvement and stabilization of unemployment rates in the United States. At the present time (June, 2019), the overall unemployment rate for the United States is 3.6 percent and has been on an improving trend over the past 12 months (Bureau of Labor Statistics n.d.-a). To remain culturally competitive, more than 75 percent of organizations have committed to creating an enhanced employment culture to boost employee engagement and organizational performance (Paterson 2014), while 65 percent of the world's leading employers have acknowledged cultural programs focused on workplace relationships, employee well-being and work–life balance are central to attracting and retaining employees (Paterson 2014). The drivers behind developing cultures focusing on well-being are associated with stress levels, organizational leadership, and coworker relations. Employers, including health care organizations, are attacking these concerns through branding programs and initiatives to strategically enhance culture, incorporating programs focused on more paid time off, more frequent breaks, safety, and flexible work options, as well as incorporating training and development opportunities (Paterson 2014). Other efforts associated with well-being and developing cultures indicate the shift in focus on the human element; 81 percent of employers aspire to develop and cultivate a culture to support productivity, employee satisfaction, and employee retention (International Council on Active Aging 2018). In 2018, 40 percent of organizations, collectively employing over five million employees, identified the significance of cultural development; up from 33 percent in 2016 (International Council on Active Aging 2018).

For health care leaders, industry employment has underscored the demand to develop strong cultures led by individuals focusing on motivation and commitment. To illustrate, within the health care services employment sector, the unemployment rate has decreased from 2.7 percent (641,000 individuals) to 2.6 percent (648,000 individuals) in the past 12 months (Bureau of Labor Statistics n.d.-a; 2018–2019) while the health care industry added approximately 368,000 jobs during the same window of time (Bureau of Labor Statistics n.d.-b). Given industry growth, the few vacancies existing in health care are in a mix of fierce competition among employers when the prior year increase in jobs has exceeded 50 percent of individuals unemployed. For health care jobs, a 2.6 percent unemployment rate accounts for 0.003 percent of unemployed health care employees and professionals (Bureau of Labor Statistics n.d.-a). In the growing health care industry, organizations are not just competing for talent, but they are competing for just over one-tenth of a percent of the unemployed industry workforce.

I say all of this to illustrate the significance of employment competition. With so much domestic competition for hiring skilled employees in not only health care, but in all industries, organizations are pressed to seek innovative approaches and strategies to ensure their employees are motivated, committed, and engaged. This includes how the employer influences organizational commitment and motivation to build a connection with employees so they stay. The difficulty in recruitment, retention, and performance places the subsequent demand on organizational culture competition.

Though commitment will be thoroughly explored later, the bottom line is that many employed individuals are passively or actively seeking alternative employment to a different organization motivated by culture, motivation, and commitment. In a study examining poorly performing cultures, approximately 75 percent of employees have identified they would leave their current organization for the "right opportunity" (Dunn 2016) It is important to understand what "right opportunity" means; it may be related to the leader, peers, benefits, or opportunities for advancement. In a 2018 study examining health care employees, the greatest employee motivators were use of personal abilities, job security, role fulfillment, and meaningful work. While motivation factors will also be discussed later, it is important to keep in mind that culture and stay intention is associated with workplace motivation. Motivation factors and culture does not completely exist in a silo, but rather as a complex and integrated force within organizations. Additionally, what motivates the sample of my studies does not necessarily mean it is congruent with all organizations. It is all about leadership focus on culture and motivation factors.

For example, when an employee is capable of leaving—or actively seeking to leave—your organization, the result may be that either the culture within is inadequate or leadership is perceived to not value culture and individual motivation factors (Dunn 2016). If motivation factors are not sufficiently understood, counterbalanced, and addressed with competing motivation factors, turnover will perpetuate because the motivation factor is inadequately satisfied. In an effort to understand turnover through motivation, internal leaders, such as our human resources professionals, seek to understand how their organizational culture is different from that of others (Dunn 2016). This includes how the organization differentiates itself in recruitment and retention activities when those efforts seem to fail (Dunn 2016). High performing leaders develop high performing cultures through understanding their culture, the motivation of their staff, and the efforts required to improve the workplace environment.

How does the organization retain and develop a team from scratch that will be successful when the employer is the independent variable in the relationship? What puts the organization above the rest in order to retain and attract the best talent and experience in the field? Simply put, a culture focused on motivation is the key to developing high performing groups. And, culture is not as simple as implementing improved programs in paid time off, work flexibility, and healthy well-being programs. Rather, a culture focused on motivation is more specific to each individual in your workforce and collective teams as many motivational factors include team related behavioral factors. It is also critically important to understand and accept the fact that turnover is not an industry phenomenon.

For health care leaders in operations, it is clear that motivation, satisfaction, and cultural development are central to employment and recruitment efforts and competition. It is essential to understand the factors associated with employees that remain with the organization and what the "right opportunity" is for those that are passively seeking alternative organizations. It is also the key to understand what organizational efforts to develop employee-centric programs look like. Is your organization developing and practicing contemporary employee engagement practices associated with flexibility and well-being programs while differentiating efforts from the competitive health care employers in the market? Is the "right opportunity" gap understood? Do leaders understand what that "right opportunity" is? What is the differentiator?

There are a multitude of motivation factors leading employees to connect or disconnect from their current employer. In an analysis of motivation factors among point-of-contact employees initiating connection with patients and customers, leading factors of motivation are outlined later. As a health care leader, how do you measure and understand the influence of motivation factors on business outcomes? The Tri-Factor Model analysis of motivation, satisfaction, and commitment, presented later, provides a foundation for identifying the weight of motivation, commitment, and satisfaction factors; all essential to understanding what leads employees to remain with an organization, as well as what draws them out to seek employment with other organizations when their needs are not met. At this early point, leaders should be prepared to evaluate and understand what motivates employees, why they stay, and what factors need to be present to drive workplace satisfaction.

Health Care Leadership Takeaways

As discussed, employee retention in modern workplace environments is driven by developing cultures focusing on motivation factors to strengthen organizational commitment. The strong unemployment rate has created a competitive landscape where health care worker unemployment is less than one-tenth of a percent.

To develop cultures, health care leaders must understand why employees stay with their organization. This includes understanding differentiating workplace benefits and programs among health care organizations and how leaders develop and commit to employee-centric environments. For employees, leaders must understand what "the right opportunity" looks like to anticipate the passive job seekers on work teams.

CHAPTER 2

Motivation

How do leaders retain and develop teams from scratch that will be successful? What positions an organization to be able to retain and attract the greatest talent? At this point, it should be clear that understanding motivation factors are the key to understanding work groups.

Workplace motivation is the force in the workplace that drives all employee behaviors and responses. Employees are motivated in different ways, requiring a comprehensive understanding of relationships in order to identify motivational needs. There should also be a level of analysis on how to counterbalance needs if they cannot be directly addressed. When employees are motivated, they exert greater levels of effort, time, and persistence to meet organizational goals. When rewards, recognition, and retention strategies do not match the workforce, the effort to address opportunities and improve focus on the human element of business fades into the background of daily busyness of management. In a health care setting, considering the fierce competition and favorable unemployment, health care leaders should understand competing components of turnover and retention.

In a case study conducted within a private sector services employer, turnover rates exceeded 50 percent. Annual turnover averaged 13.7 employees per day. Exit interviews indicated that the organization was considered a favorable employer among 72.3 percent of participants. Of these participants, 57 percent were employed less than 2 years, 40 percent were employed two to five years, and 3 percent were employed for greater than 5 years. Of the respondents, 82 percent reported strong teamwork, 42 percent left the employer due to higher paying employment, 38 percent left for "something else," 12 percent left because of poor management, and 8 percent left because of physical demands. Results are presented in Figures 2.1 and 2.2.

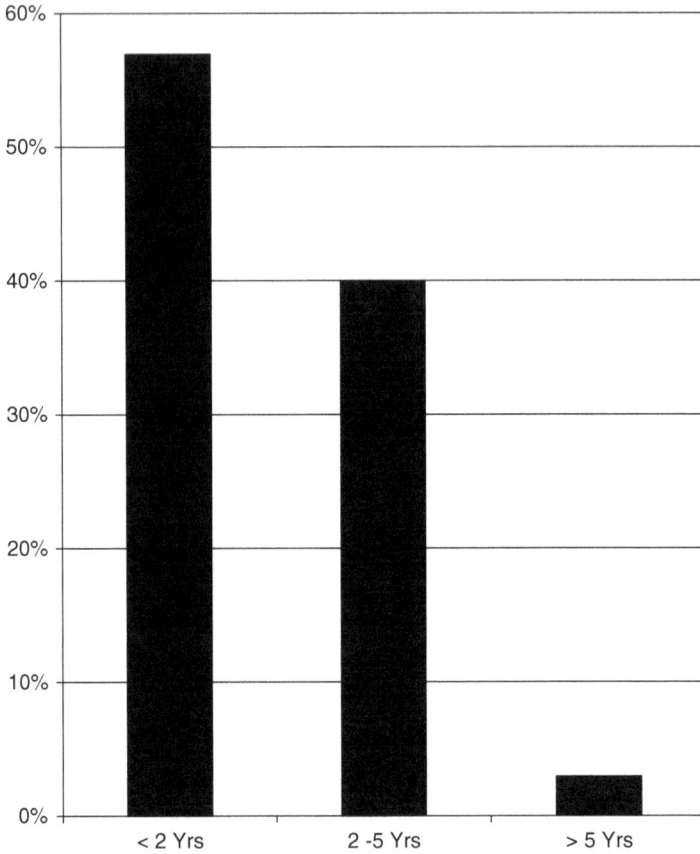

Figure 2.1 **Private sector service organizational duration**
of employment

In examining motivation factors, pay and salary generally surfaces from health care leaders as a leading factor, though data and evidence of this is often lacking. Understanding the counterbalance of factors is essential to address such factors and consideration of pay as a factor. Pay is an extrinsic motivation factor while peer interactions and relationships are intrinsic motivation factors. The organization in the case study primarily has driven employee engagement in intrinsic factors of role fulfillment, advancement, development, and a culture of caring. These factors are important and effective components of culture and motivation. However, the organization in the case study miserably failed to address or counterbalance compensation-related motivational

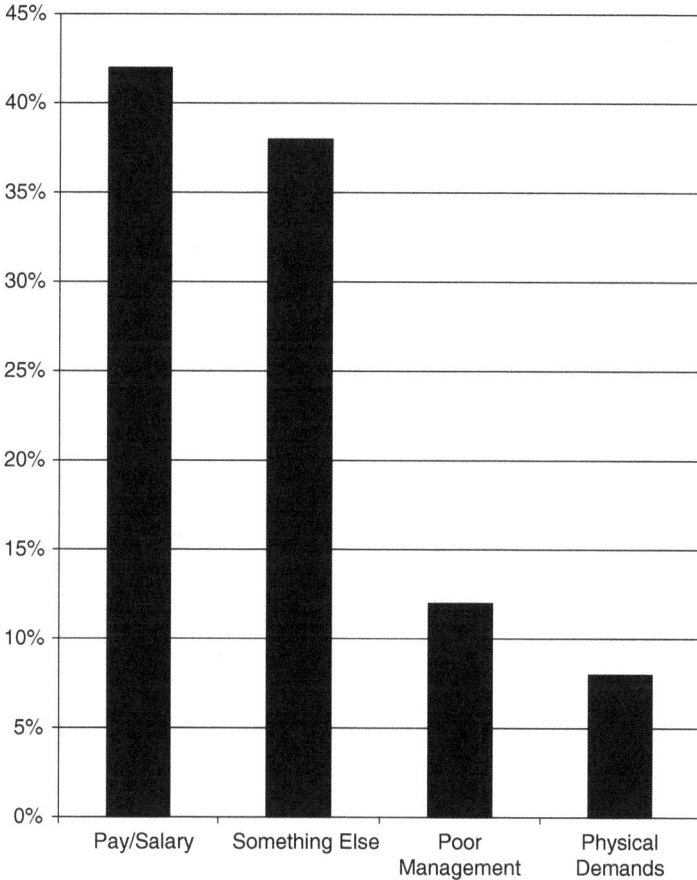

Figure 2.2 Private sector service organization—reason for leaving the organization

factors evidenced by the analysis. The identification of factors and motivators suggests that though employees are intrinsically motivated, stay intention is based on extrinsic motivation. Extrinsic motivators include supervisory relationships, leadership styles, working conditions, role status, and job security. If employees are extrinsically motivated to remain with an employer, turnover will not improve when the organization is performing very well in intrinsic motivation factors and very poorly on extrinsic motivation.

In a setting where pay is among the greatest motivation factors identified, how can the organization seek to mitigate turnover on pay-related factors? Nearly half of the workforce was employed for more than 2 years.

There is a cost of knowledge, cost of performance, and the investment of training to replace long-term employees. Clearly, a significant amount of financial *expenditures* (not to be confused with *investment*, in this case) have been utilized to continually recruit and employ individuals that are not likely to remain with this organization. Again: *expenditures to recruit individuals unlikely to remain with the employer.* Imagine constantly driving a car, burning gas to go where you have already been for the sake and purpose of burning more gas. Extrinsic motivation, in this instance, is where the focus should be for the case study organization. Financial resources are consistently being spent to recruit employees who are not going to stay, rather than investing in balancing motivation factors with a largely favorable culture.

While motivation and organizational commitment will be reviewed later in a manner that supports this outcome, an organization that loses an average of 13.7 employees per day is alarming. This is especially concerning when those exiting the organization felt it was a pleasant place to work through teamwork and peer interaction while the most turnover occurred because of pay or other reasons. Employee exit interviews comprising such data suggest a significant demand for investigating motivation factors within the workforce.

All of that aside, motivation depends on employees' perceptions and attitudes of their employer; the relationship between motivation, perception, and attitude influences organizational commitment. Motivation, and the extent to which an employee identifies with an organization, mediates organizational commitment as it is driven by intrinsic and extrinsic motivation factors. When lower levels of motivation factors, either intrinsic or extrinsic motivation, are present, organizational commitment is weaker and declines, as evidenced in the spiraling turnover in the prior case study. These factors are presented through Herzberg's (1959) model of workplace motivation factors.

Workplace Motivation Theory

Background

Herzberg's 1959 motivation theory has been identified by contemporary and seminal research as an effective method to understand workplace motivation (Costello and Welch 2014) Herzberg's model of corporate employee satisfaction analysis proposed evaluating both motivation and hygiene factors. Motivating (intrinsic) factors support satisfaction and motivation (Table 2.1) by incorporating achievement, recognition, empathetic and caring environments, work relevance, and growth opportunities (extrinsic). Employees do not attempt to improve unless intrinsic factors are present and evident in their environment.

Table 2.1 Herzberg's motivation factors

Factor	Motivation	Factor type
Achievement	Task completion, early completion	Motivation (Intrinsic): Positive presence of the factor has a satisfaction and motivational influence on workers
Recognition	Benefits of performance, monetary or nonmonetary	
The Work Itself	Essence of work performed contributing, and contributable to contentment	
Responsibility	Autonomy to perform a task, individual terms in making a decision as to how work is carried out	
Advancement	Increased responsibility, status, and financial benefits	
Growth	Opportunity to learn new skills	

Researchers have found, in multiple environments, that factors of workforce motivation are complicated; individual needs vary based on attitude, perceptions, education level, and personality (Kotni and Karumuri 2018). Intrinsic motivational factors lead to increased individual output with a positive effect on morale, productivity, satisfaction, and efficiency (Kotni and Karumuri 2018). Dissatisfaction among employees may result from the absence of extrinsic factors in company policy, administration, supervision, interpersonal relationships, salary, job security, personal life, working conditions, and job status. Positive extrinsic factors have been identified in salary, nature of the job, company policies, and procedures (Kotni and Karumuri 2018). On the other hand, reimbursements, pay increases, employment terms, job security, and peer relations provided mixed results in motivation as such factors are largely extrinsic.

Motivation, Education, and Skill-Level Variance

In a recent study to illustrate differences in workforce skill and education levels, a survey of administrative staff at universities using an instrument to evaluate satisfaction in pay, promotion, supervision, fringe and contingent rewards, working conditions, coworkers, communications, and nature of the work, was conducted (Katenova et al. 2016). Respondents were satisfied with supervision, nature of work, and coworkers but dissatisfied with working conditions and pay (extrinsic factors in Herzberg's theory). Researchers provided an empirical approach to evaluating hygiene and motivator factors with the same terms as intrinsic and extrinsic factors, explored the potential significance of skill and education levels, and connected commitment factors to Herzberg's theory of motivation (Katenova et al. 2016). Additional research surfaced in studying various hospitality studies. Results of the study indicated that different roles had different motivating factors (further outlined in Table 2.2). For the complex environment and significant variance in education and skill levels among employees, leaders must understand the motivation factors of the employees they lead.

Consistently, in the health care service worker study presented in Chapter 6, a significant amount of research exists in examining the relationships between motivation and organizational commitment. However, it is exceedingly rare for commitment and motivation to be observed among frontline, lesser-educated employee workgroups. Through evaluating motivation factors, Herzberg's (1959) approach was used as it postulated that intrinsic and extrinsic motivation factors influence workplace satisfaction. Intrinsic factors drive emotional and cognitive reactions to achievement, recognition, opportunities for promotion and advancement, the nature of the job, satisfaction, and responsibility. Extrinsic factors include salary, working conditions, supervision, social status, peer relationships, and job security. Job satisfaction and dissatisfaction are opposing dimensions influenced by intrinsic motivating factors and dissatisfying hygiene factors (Vijayakumar and Saxena 2015). In contemporary literature, a relationship between motivation and organizational commitment

Table 2.2 *Leading positive motivation factors among health care workers*

Physicians/MDs (Allen 2017; Ratanawongsa et al. 2006)	Nursing/RNs (Dzaher 2017; LaFerney 2018)	Technicians/entry-level (Johnson 2019a)	Administrative support roles (Johnson 2019a)
The role itself	The role itself	The role itself	The role itself
Role fulfillment	Role fulfillment	Role fulfillment	
Job security	Job security/demand	Job Security	
Salary	Salary		Salary
Autonomy			
Relationships with leadership		Relationship with supervisor	Relationship with supervisor
Purpose	Purpose	Purpose	
Challenge			
Accomplishment	Accomplishment		
Relationships with peers	Relationships with peers	Relationships with peers	Relationships with peers
Self-expression			
Status	Status		
		Supervisor competency	Supervisor competency

has been consistently identified and observed (Ozturk et al. 2016; Potipiroon and Ford 2017; Tosun and Ulusoy 2017). Correlations between affective organizational commitment and intrinsic and extrinsic motivation factors among nurses and physicians has also been observed, supporting the presence of intrinsic factors (e.g., work meaningfulness and fulfillment; Tosun and Ulusoy 2017). Findings consistently support positive relationships with affective organizational commitment (Tosun and Ulusoy 2017). Extrinsic factors (e.g., job demands and stressors) have inverse relationships with affective organizational commitment (Tosun and Ulusoy 2017). Consistently observed, it has been identified that affective commitment (i.e., the emotional connection and attachment between employees and employers) has a negative relationship with extrinsic motivator factors and a positive relationship with intrinsic factors (Ozturk et al. 2016).

Aspects of industry and the nature of employment have further been found to influence motivating factors; motivation influences work-related behaviors, performance intensity, and employment duration (Lundberg et al. 2009). Researchers have suggested that motivation and organizational commitment influence employee turnover, organizational effectiveness, and employee job satisfaction (Daw and Khoury 2014). In other words, motivation factors have a strong causal relationship with employee turnover and stay intention. Employees with lower levels of satisfaction and motivation feel less committed to their employer, have higher levels of turnover intention, and exhibit decreased individual performance. There, as presented later in a study, is a need for a structured approach to develop a better understanding of how motivation factors within the workplace influence organizational commitment. Motivation factors are listed in Tables 2.1, 2.2, and 2.3. Components of leadership influence are outlined in Table 2.4.

Health Care Leadership Takeaways

As a leader in health care, the factors given in Table 2.3 are found to be most prominent among roles. But, how does a leader support and influence these factors? There are both supportive and adverse behaviors leaders can exhibit to develop a more robust culture, improve workplace motivation, and foster organizational commitment. Table 2.4 outlines these factors.

Table 2.3 Leading demotivating factors among health care workers

Physicians/MDs (Ratanawongsa et al. 2006)	Nursing/RNs (LaFerney 2018)	Technicians/ entry-level (Johnson 2019b)	Administrative support roles
Education debt			
Compensation delay			
Training required			
Cost of malpractice			
Time constraints	Time constraints		
Long hours	Long hours		
Work–life balance			
		Pay	Pay
		Limited alternative employment options	Limited alternative employment options
		Personal investment	
	Performance hindrances/ processes/policies	Performance hindrances/processes/ policies	Workplace policies
		Workplace competition	Workplace COMPETITION
			Working conditions

Table 2.4 Motivation factors and leader influence

Motivation factor definition	Supportive leader factors	Adverse leader factors
Goal achievement: The extent to which employees have the ability and autonomy to identify and prioritize objectives and activities leading to a goal.	Providing tasks and objectives as goals to employees in a manner that allows for creativity and autonomy in how employees choose to accomplish directives.	Specific step-by-step prescriptive direction connecting idea or task to completion. Telling competent employees how to achieve goals for a specific task.

(continued)

Motivation factor definition	Supportive leader factors	Adverse leader factors
The work itself: A complex motivation factor described as the extent to which the work assigned to an individual has purpose, meaning, and positive self-perceptions.	Working with employees to identify the types of work that motivate them in their workplace, setting goals for attaining and providing the proper training and education to reach the role.	Placing employees into roles without understanding how the role influences their motivation; failure to review job satisfaction and progress with the employee.
Relationship with supervisor: One of the most influential motivation factors in the workplace moving employees to sacrifice personal advantages for the sake of a leader.	Open mediums for communications, individual one-on-one activities (lunch, stay interviews, etc.), providing and sticking to follow-up for employee needs (set a date, commit to serving employees), servant leadership, transformational leadership.	Assumptive behaviors that one-way communication indicates a supportive environment (*saying* they have an open door, or *saying* they are always available), not learning about employees, failure to regularly check in, failure to understand what motivates each employee.
Salary: An extrinsic motivation factor defined by the extent to which an individual is motivated by monetary need or status.	Communicating and enabling a culture that acknowledges the value one brings to his or her role, employer and customers, considering the small incremental adjustments for 'big wins' with employees, understanding personal motivating reasons to be motived by salary.	Failure to celebrate performance achievement and valuable contribution, budget "rigidity," losing focus of the human element of being a leader, failure to be subjective with emotionally based and situational-based motivation for salary.
Control over role: Pertains to the level of influence and input one holds over his or her schedule, sequence of tasks, tools and methods used and deadline influence.	Allowing employees the opportunity to determine how they will achieve performance objectives, follow-up on how their choices supported performance.	Maintaining a strict and rigid workplace with highly structured job flows without considering and seeking employee feedback on how the job flow could be improved, or how they would change it if they had the opportunity to do so.

Motivation factor definition	Supportive leader factors	Adverse leader factors
Supervisor quality: The perception and extent to which an employee identifies competency in job skill and interpersonal skill.	Servant leadership, follow-up to concerns, self-education on management skills and employee leadership skills, training staff on proper approaches and shadowing followers for task comprehension.	Exerting power authority, over exertion of position influence perception projecting, failure to being open to learning tasks and keeping up with company changes, failure to hold knowledge influence.
Role fulfillment: Refers to how we socially play our parts, or *roles*, that social settings expect and how we feel fit and aligned with those roles.	Breaking tasks down into categories among staff to understand what most motivates them about their role, additional training and development for enhancing employee motivation role tasks, structuring positions around motivating work.	Failure to realize employees perform less effectively when engaging in tasks with lower motivation and intrinsic value, position and structure rigidity that does not permit flexing of tasks and roles to meet employee motivation needs, failure to understand that employees who are not motivated by their role function will leave your organization for more fulfilling work.
Purpose: The extent to which an employee feels emotionally connected to his or her role, peers, culture, leader and organization.	Soliciting employees for motivations and skills to uniquely contribute to the team and organization, developing a culture of shared expertise and motivation where employees share the skills they have and the skills they need/depend on, embracing the fact that employees have specific motivation triggers that, when used, create higher performance, retention, satisfaction, and engagement.	Managing departments and employees by a strict culture of adherence to roles, failure to engage staff on what their goals are, failure to understand what intrinsically motivates each employee, failure to one-on-one solicit feedback from employees on motivating tasks.

(continued)

Motivation factor definition	Supportive leader factors	Adverse leader factors
Limited alternative employment options: A motivation factor that influences individual and personal behavior. In settings where there are limited alternative options for employment, employees feel "stuck." If employees do not have options within their workplace for task and role variety, the limited alternative employment options hold greater weight and demotivate individuals through a lack of intrinsically driven motivation factors.	Evaluating if the "right person" is in the "right role" for him or her as a human, providing learning for skills that are not directly related to the tasks an employee carries out daily in order to develop skills for him or her to seek advancement or lateral role change in his or her organization, embracing employees with value and appreciation to influence role fulfillment and purpose.	Holding position rigidity, failure to understand what roles employees would like to move into, acknowledging the skill and motivation gap but not responding in a supportive way, failure to realize that turnover influences the entire organization due to the loss of a potentially developed employee for other roles.
Personal investment: The extent to which an employee feels like he or she has invested so much time and energy that he or she cannot attain or readily produce the same outputs in another organization. His or her efforts have plateaued to a level of workplace exertion exhaustion.	Publicly and personally sharing appreciation for the commitment an employee has demonstrated, seeking additional ways an employee would like to expand his or her role or potential, celebrating milestones, and significant achievements.	Acknowledging investment and efforts while failing to seek ways and roles in which an employee can continue to exert the same energy toward another role or task, failure to realize that personal investment has a limited capacity until employees begin to give less due to no changes correlated to the exertion they have expended.
Performance hindrances: Refers to the extent to which barriers demotivate employees. Examples include policies prohibiting promotions in terms of time, limited budgets to provide necessary tools, local competition, economic dynamics and emerging trends. All factors provide limitations on how one can conduct his or her own work and be positively motivated.	Considering flexing prohibitive policies that "lock" employees into unfavorable circumstances that are undue, evaluating the influence political and budgetary models and cultures that influence how employees are able to complete work, working one-on-one with employees to identify ways they can influence how to better perform in their role.	Policy and budget rigidity, failure to properly plan for needs and industry/organizational changes, failure to solicit feedback on how a job can be better designed for performance, acknowledging the feedback and not following up with how, why and "'if" changes may be made to improve performance capacity.

Source: Johnson (2019b).

CHAPTER 3

Organizational Commitment

Organizational commitment is measured as the bond an employee holds with his or her employer. Organizational commitment and workplace motivation interact in a direct correlational manner. In this chapter, organizational commitment will be introduced as we continue to discover the process of building a cultural driven workplace that supports employee retention, performance, and motivation. The primary focus is on that of affective organizational commitment. Affective organizational commitment is based on the positive and motivating emotional connection motivating employees to proactively serve their employer in ways that deliberately improve organizational performance, support positive relationships within the organization, and increase overall emotional connectedness (Lapointe and Vandenberghe 2018).

Within health care, patient experience goals emerge as a performance indicator, making this connection essential to understanding the link between culture and performance. Though organizations have been developing their own cultures, vision, and values, value-based management has developed as a concept for value development and leadership (Ortega-Parra and Sastre-Castillo 2013). With varying initiatives, employees respond in different ways to these various motives, leading to a need for uniformity in bringing widely held values in line with social trends, supporting the links between corporate culture and organizational commitment (Ortega-Parra and Sastre-Castillo 2013).

Comprehensive models of cultural factors and connections to health care roles, including definitions and characteristics of the health care environment, have been posed in the human element and the technical nature of health care settings. For health care leaders, enhancing leading commitment factors in the health care environment, including employee commitment and human treatment, improving components of health care delivery, including technical care, interpersonal relationships, and environment; and each of these are essential to building the foundation of commitment (Ortega et al. 2015). Health care employees are, generally, more intrinsically motivated by job purpose and job fulfillment in the delivery of care and services to patients, which influences organizational commitment. Motivators that support organizational commitment depend on relationship-oriented behaviors, such as a caring atmosphere, communication, patient-centeredness, courtesy, dignity, and humanism (Katenova et al. 2016). As outlined in Chapter 2, health care leaders can influence these factors to build motivation through supportive and adverse behavior.

Organizational commitment is based on the theoretical foundation from Katz (1951) where organizational commitment was described as how workers enter and withdraw from workgroups due to their ability to make decisions within workgroups (Katz 1951). Organizational commitment is based on three definitive behavioral responses to how an individual emotionally identifies and connects with his or her employer. First, *affective organizational commitment* is described as the emotional attachment, identification with, and involvement employees have with their organizations (McShane et al. 2009). Second, *continuance organizational commitment* is based on necessity and personal sacrifice to remain with an employer because of limitations and alternative options (Lapointe and Vandenberghe 2018). Limitations can be the result of geographic limitations, minimal education and skills, and the need to provide for a family or other support requirement. And, lastly, *normative organizational commitment* depends on the employee's sense of loyalty, obligation, and commitment to membership providing valuable benefits from belonging to or being part of an organization (Lapointe and Vandenberghe 2018).

The focus on motivation and commitment within this book identifies ways to improve affective organizational commitment through intentionally balancing intrinsic and extrinsic motivation factors. The study on health care service worker motivation and commitment identifies, within the specific workgroup, how intrinsic motivation may be enhanced in order to improve correlations in affective organizational commitment to improve turnover, retention, and both employee and organizational performance. Affective commitment leads employees to actively support and serve their employer in a deliberate manner to contribute to organizational performance, supporting positive relationships while overall enhancing emotional connectedness (Lapointe and Vandenberghe 2018). Essentially, through psychological attachment, affective organizational commitment leads employees to desire to see organizational success through their own personal contributions (Khera 2017). When organizational commitment is weak, consequences include employee absence, turnover, performance deficiencies, lower citizenship behaviors, work-related stress, and conflict. Emotional attachment, stay intention, meaningful work, and connection have been identified as positively correlating with organization influences on affective commitment in developing motivation factors of social dynamics and peer relations (Luo et al. 2018).

Perceived Culture and Organizational Commitment

In addition to identifying motivation factors, evaluating perceived culture provides additional insight into organizational commitment. Perceived culture is a set of deeply held values, meanings, and beliefs within an organization. Commitment and perceptions of informal rules and beliefs in an environment relate to individual behaviors, so long as the workplace culture aligns with employee behaviors and operational business outcomes. The development of individual behaviors involves interrelated factors of perceived behavioral control, attitudes, and subjective norms. Organizational commitment reflects personal, job-related, and organizational variables. Commitment, as the measure of an employee's affiliation with an organization, creates a binding force influencing behaviors in ways that are relevant to organizational objectives. Committed employees are more likely to be active, productive, and exhibit behaviors that support the interests of their employer through positive motivation effects on commitment, including job autonomy, complexity, and training (Spanuth and Wald 2017). Health care leaders can support these behaviors embracing and thoroughly understanding employee motivation among their teams to create a more harmonious workplace.

Commitment and Relationship Factors

Organizational commitment and workplace relationship factors among peers and leaders (intrinsic motivation factor) have causal relationships with organizational commitment and organizational trust. Commitment mediates employee behavior when expectations of rewards for performance are understood (intrinsic motivation factor; Iannuzzi et al. 2015). Employees are more likely to contribute to an organization in which they belong and are more likely to consult others for assistance (intrinsic motivation factor). The mediating role of commitment and organization support is that employees gain higher levels of identification if employers treat them fairly. Commitment is positively related to knowledge-sharing behaviors, fairness, identification, and collaboration with peers. Employees develop stronger commitment bonds and weaker instrumental ties (e.g., justice, fairness, respect, and support) when leaders are receptive to suggestions in a fair and reliable manner.

The relationship between commitment and satisfaction has been investigated to discover whether participants had higher than average affective commitment despite high burnout levels in a health care setting. Desensitization to the workplace environment was average, intrinsic satisfaction was high (due to personal successes), and extrinsic satisfaction was low (Tosun and Ulusoy 2017). The commitment of an employee to an organization affects business outcomes. In a health care setting, employee satisfaction improves patient satisfaction and quality of care. Research has identified a positive relationship between affective commitment and job satisfaction and a negative relationship between continuance commitment and job satisfaction (Tosun and Ulusoy 2017).

Additional studies have examined the relationship between culture, satisfaction, and organizational change to identify commitment via causal factors associated with job characteristics, leadership, and job fulfillment. Such studies have sampled nurses in general hospital wards, psychiatric wards, and private wards and found that the level of control over the working environment had the highest correlation with commitment and employee satisfaction (Lok and Crawford 2017).

Past researchers developed four models to examine the relationship between commitment and satisfaction: (1) job satisfaction leads to commitment, (2) commitment leads to satisfaction, (3) satisfaction and commitment affect each other, and (4) commitment and satisfaction are independent (Aksoy et al. 2018). There is a positive relationship between satisfaction and affective commitment and a weak relationship between satisfaction and continuance commitment. This view provides a framework for evaluating the influence of satisfaction on commitment and confirmed the need to focus on each factor in tandem with other environmental factors. Organizations must provide psychological support and meet the social needs of employees (i.e., motivation factors). Employee commitment increases if organizations enhance employees' relationships with their organization by fostering motivation through shared values, congruence, and relations. Health care leaders can support commitment through job satisfaction.

Organizational Practice

A critical aspect for the studies presented later existing in the dimension of organizational culture includes the impact of commitment to organizational practice, values, and performance. Research has revealed links between corporate culture and commitment, particularly when considering the relationship with organizational performance (Ortega-Parra and Sastre-Castillo 2013). As outlined, within health care, patient experience goals have emerged as a key performance indicator. The connection between performance components is essential to understanding the link between culture and performance. While organizations independently and naturally develop their own cultures, vision, and values, leadership and management focused on employee values has developed as an approach to being more effective (Ortega-Parra and Sastre-Castillo 2013). Varying initiatives lead employees to respond in different ways to various motives, demanding a need for uniformity in bringing widely held values in line with organizational challenges, supporting operational goals and objectives while also supporting links between culture and commitment (Ortega-Parra and Sastre-Castillo 2013).

Regarding employee behavior, culture influences context and develops environments for clues for authentic behaviors. A culture of authenticity supports engagement, motivation, fulfillment, and a state of mind that supports the emotional feeling that employees are engaged in activities that fit their core values in ways congruent with their core selves. Essentially, organizational culture has the potential to drive influence in employee engagement in ways that may encourage employees to participate in authentic behaviors in the workplace. Moreover, authenticity has been associated with increased self-esteem and well-being, leading to decreased workplace stress, depression, and turnover (Reis et al. 2016). Since culture encompasses shared values and assumptions guiding meaningful behaviors and relationships in the workplace, expected standards of behavior emerge as proper ways to thinking and feeling in the workplace, regulating emotional expressions.

Health Care Leadership Takeaways

A culture of authenticity has been identified as a leading driver of employee engagement and is supported by leadership integrity, transparency, and clear motives. Health care leaders can support and develop cultures of authenticity through self-awareness of one's own strengths, limitations, and values. Leaders can also build this through transparency, demonstrating honesty and straightforward behaviors, fair-minded practices soliciting viewpoints and consistently "doing the right thing." These behaviors are also outlined in Chapter 2. Similarly, leaders can build organizational commitment by creating a culture of teamwork, transparency, trust, and innovation. Leaders that also seek feedback from employees support affective organizational commitment by involving staff and capitalizing on their individual investments in their workplace and employer.

CHAPTER 4

Culture, Subculture, and Attribution

Organizational culture is a behavioral web composed of shared beliefs and values among workgroups, individuals, and the overall organization. This web holds varying degrees of influence on employees and groups where, as outlined later, cultural factors can be shown to consistently and uniformly exist with dependency. Likewise, cultural independence can be identified where workgroups hold cultural measures and motivational factors which are not consistent with the larger organization or other similar groups. As an example, a cultural analysis of one hospital compared to the parent health system may collectively be consistent with the rest of the organization. However, within work groups, differences may exist to varying degrees between like groups. The cultural and motivational factors of an intensive care unit (ICU) nursing team at Hospital A can be significantly different from an ICU nursing team at Hospital B, though the overall hospital is consistent with the overall parent health system.

The differences across a health system in subgroups can include components of engagement, such as employer loyalty and pride, understanding contributions to success, group cohesion and effectiveness, embracing organizational mission and vision, and accessibility to resources to perform one's role. Varying differences can influence how employees work together, how they embrace the organization's purpose and mission, how they embrace training and development, and how they support their manager. As a leader, understanding these differences as pockets of subculture provides a foundation to identification of motivation factors and satisfaction aspects to improve team performance. Each team is motivated by, and responds differently to, different workplace factors. Independent groups must be handled in a way that addresses motivation, satisfaction, and commitment as it specifically applies to the independent group, rather than the organization as a whole.

Culture is, locally or systemically, shaped by discourse and behaviors with other employees and individuals in the organization and includes management influence. Culture is further shaped by the larger environment pressures from the overall organization (much like the health system and hospital example in the preceding text), internal member interactions, and operational objectives. Operational objectives are among the most significant influencing factors on organizational culture. And, individual motivation is influenced by employer objectives. That being said, there are three interrelated components to culture: motivation factors, organizational objectives, and individual interactions. Subcomponents of organizational culture include perceived factors, attribution, and behavioral clues for how one may behaviorally fit into the environment, or detract from the environment. Figures 4.1, 4.2, and 4.3 outline cultural interactions.

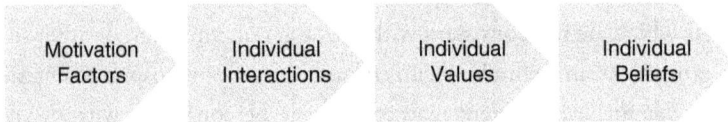

Figure 4.1 *Individual culture integration*

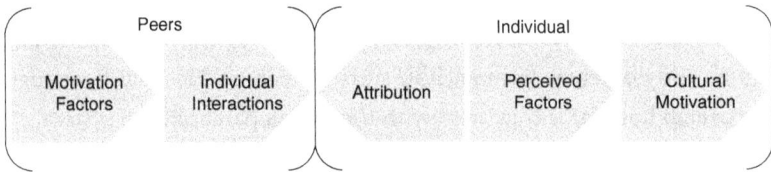

Figure 4.2 *Cultural integration and motivation*

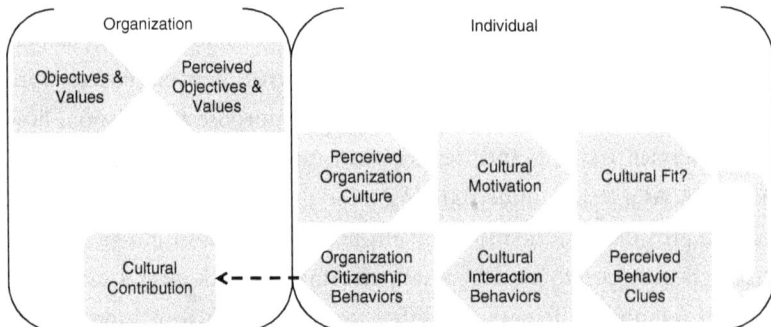

Figure 4.3 *Behavioral culture integration*

For leaders, understanding the phases employees go through within workgroups and culture integration and contribution provides insight to the level to which an employee is integrated. Further, understanding group and individual motivation factors allows managers to identify which factors to apply while observing group interactions and progress in assimilating employees to work groups.

Figure 4.1 illustrates the transition that driving individual integration into a culture is first driven by motivation factors. Motivation factors influence individual interactions. For example, employees that are intrinsically motivated may be motivated by peer relationships. The interactions hold a relationship with individual values by way of individual interaction consistency with motivation factors and what consistency exists in cultural values and individual values. Individual beliefs are influenced by individual values where motivation shapes value and value supports a belief structure or stance. Employee motivation within an environment of interactions that are consistent with their values and beliefs results in the integration of the employee into the culture, contributing to the organizational environment. It should be noted that cultural contribution that is based on motivation factors and environment consistency does not equate to positive cultural contribution. Clearly, not all workplace cultures are positive environments; an extrinsically motivated employee in an organization sharing similar motivations may not possess positive intrinsically motivated behaviors.

In a slightly different view, cultural integration can be motivated by environmental factors when employees seek to identify and understand peers in their environment before being motivated by the culture. In Figure 4.2, the initial observations and influencing factors are based on work peer values and beliefs. As an individual observes these factors, he or she formulates assumptions and attributes to the environment. Once such assumptions are formulated by a perceived reality of what is truly behaviorally present in the environment, motivation is influenced by the perceived culture. Cultural motivation may come, as outlined previously, through intrinsic and, or, extrinsic factor presence. While Figure 4.1 identifies an individual journey into a culture, Figure 4.2 provides a framework where the environment of peers determines perceptions, attribution, and subsequent motivation and behavioral outcomes.

Extending the cultural integration and motivation model in Figure 4.2, Figure 4.3 provides a model of behavioral integration into a culture. Essentially, organizational objectives and values shape the perception an individual forms that is then either positively or negatively motivating. Cultural fit, as determined by the level of motivational consistency, leads individuals to contribute, or withdraw from, behavioral integration into the culture. When individuals integrate into a culture, behavior is driven by the clues within an environment mediating employee behavior, determining what behavior is right, wrong, acceptable, or unacceptable. This is the process whereby the employee goes through a norming phase, enhancing cultural interaction behaviors. Once the employee has gone through the norming portion of culture interactions and behaviors, organizational citizenship behaviors begin to develop and occur. When an employee commits to organizational culture and behavior, a contribution to the culture occurs. Again, contribution may be positive or negative, based on the specific motivations of the employee, employer, peers, and overall consistency.

Finally, in Figure 4.4, it is important to outline the relationship between an external individual and an external employer. Think about the

Figure 4.4 Employee–employer motivational alignment

organizations that you personally are most attracted to—and *why*. Consider highly ethical companies or social contribution companies. Conversely, think of destructive, unethical, and socioeconomic crippling organizations. The community I currently live in has a utilities organization with a true nature and conservation-oriented approach to contributing back to the environment. The organization, in the dead of winter when the ground is sufficiently frozen, deploys a machine that resembles an army tank into the marshy bottoms of riverways and lakes. The vehicle is designed to result in minimal disturbance of the habitat, and is used to travel to remote locations to build structures and habitats for local migratory waterfowl to nest in when they migrate back to the state in spring. The company does not market this behavior, nor does the activity occur in populated areas. On the other hand, there are endless examples of companies that have acted with little integrity and social care. For example, current news is focused on the Boeing 737 Max 8 aircraft that was put into service in mid-2017. After concerns about the safety of the plane, pilot reports on controllability of the aircraft, and two deadly crashes killing more than 300 people minutes after taking off, Boeing held a position that the aircraft was safe. After being grounded by the National Travel Safety Board, Boeing acknowledged there were safety concerns of the 737 Max 8. It is clear that trust, confidence, and integrity came into question among one of the world's leading transportation manufacturing organizations.

To illustrate the relationship between external employees and external employers (from an employment perspective), individuals hold motivation factors to varying degrees. The organizational values hold a relationship with individual motivation factors. For example, if an employee is motivated by social contributions, he or she will be motivated to work for—and support—such organizations. The efforts of a health care leader can influence this through sufficiently marketing core company purpose, values, the mission, and the organizational philosophy to recruit and attract the greatest fitting staff. The objective is to hire the best fitting employees for the environment, culture, teams, and groups. Think of the organization TOMS Shoes and how they position themselves publicly. For every pair of shoes sold, the organization sends a free pair of shoes to a community in need of shoes. The behaviors of motivation among employees is also directly related to—and motivated by—the organizational objectives. If the individual is motivated by contributions to nature, natural resources, and land conservation, a natural resources-dependent organization may be negatively perceived, such as a water bottling company building a collection site tapping into a protected river or water source. It is these behaviors of the organization that have consistency or inconsistency with external individuals, determining the motivation of individuals associated with organizational actions and outcomes. In terms of relationships between external employers and external employees, leaders should anticipate the needs of potential employees and the culture, purpose, mission and philosophy of the organization.

Subcultures

Subcultures are a critical component to both overall culture and organizational leadership, particularly when acknowledging and managing the existence of counterculture. Within culture, there are varying connections to power in subcultures. Subcultures are groups within the organization exhibiting patterns of behaviors and hold values largely consistent with the organization while countercultures exhibit behavior, indicating rejection of the organizational behavior, values, and social system (Uhl-Bien et al. 2014). On the surface, social influence and advantages through sources and kinds of power seem to come into play for subcultures. If the group exhibits supportive behaviors, their actions and commitment would lend to a stronger position and consideration for changes and control in the organizational environment.

As an example, leaders can forge subcultures with workgroups sharing motivation factors. If a team is motivated by growth and advancement, the leader can provide opportunities specific to that work group to satisfy this motivation. This can, in turn, improve and influence performance for the group. For a supporting behavior, the subculture supports the overall organization by acquiring new skills and knowledge to improve the overall company. This lends to subculture dependence.

Cultural dependence comes into play as organizations benefit from subcultures. The power influence comes from needs and access that influence an aspect of another person or group, including information, decisions, and assignments. Dependence also comes from control over access to wants and needs that the organization depends on within subcultures to embrace and exhibit to drive effective performance while minimizing potential adverse outcomes of counterculture groups. This is especially true considering the level of power by association and connection from the subculture and organizational leadership. To have a higher level of influence as a team of positively influencing and positively performing members, a counterculture likely will hold less power, omitting any dependence—and thus, control. Think about an organization that is rapidly growing.

A health care organization I was a part of was growing through responding to service needs more rapidly than the organization was able to grow and promote talent. This is not a rare occurrence in health care. For example, a 500 bed hospital may only have 250 patients because they do not have the human resources to open the rest of the hospital. To couple the troubled situation, consider the same rapidly growing organization working to motivate employees to participate in training and development opportunities. In such a case, the motivational needs for organizations are employees motivated by growth, training, and development in order to support operating demands. Leaders can influence this by anticipating organizational needs, offering opportunities, and influencing related motivation factors.

The alternative to embracing and motivating cultural need can result in countercultures. Countercultures can easily develop in a high demand situation such as an explosion of growth and ever increasing demands. However, subcultures can also quickly develop to support workforce development. From a leadership perspective, the supporters within the overall culture become the cheerleaders who are capable of influencing the rest of the workforce in a positive and objective supporting manner. Equally impactful, leaders within subcultures also drive commitment on the employee level by improving job satisfaction and organizational commitment behaviors and contributing to improved organizational performance.

Ultimately, subcultures may hold values, behaviors, and norms with varying degrees of alignment with the organization's overall operating culture. For leadership and management, it is critical to acknowledge and understand that subcultures are typically stronger than operating cultures. Consequently, with subcultures holding such strong positions on a more independent level within the overall organization, clashes may surface and cause problems with implementations of strategies and change; subcultures emerge as the new "sheriff in town." Subcultures, in terms of performance can either positively or adversely influence the organization in quality, service behaviors, internal teamwork, and collaboration.

Attribution

While motivation, commitment, and culture have been extensively covered thus far, I want to cover the subject of attribution and Attribution Theory. Attribution is an extremely powerful behavioral construct with significant behavioral outputs. Attribution theory describes how individuals interpret events within their environment and how attributes relate to thinking and behavior (Weiner 2019). The basis of Attribution Theory is that individuals attempt to determine why people behave in particular ways based on a three-stage process: (1) the individual has to observe and perceive the behavior, (2) the individual has to believe the behavior observed was intentionally performed, and (3) the individual must determine if the behavior observed was forced (situational attribution) or not (personal attribution; Weiner 2019). Attribution involves ability, effort, task difficulty, and perceived luck for achievement, and it is classified along the dimensions of locus of control, individual stability, and internal controllability (Weiner 2019).

In attribution, causal attributions determine affective reactions. If an employee believes that a specific manager only provides recognition for a specific type of behavior, then the employee will (when consistent in motivation factors) specifically seek to sufficiently meet the behavior warranting reward. On the individual level, employees often attribute success to factors of education, working long hours, successfully completing projects, and participating in organizational initiatives. From a motivational perspective, if an employee is intrinsically motivated on factors associated with attribution of effort, leaders lose a large amount of managerial influence and factor motivation. If employees attribute factors related to certain outcomes (including leader interactions), motivation becomes difficult to navigate. Further, if leaders exhibit specific behaviors associated with organizational citizenship or mandated actions, employees may attribute behaviors to integrity, leadership charisma, as well as leader and organizational values. Hence, it is critically important to internalize and understand the demonstration of behaviors among employees. Such attribution of behaviors can develop cultural responses that are inaccurate with cultural clues for behavior and cultural integration.

CHAPTER 5

Health Care Organizational Culture Disruption Case Study

In late 2016, an organizational behavior-focused study was conducted at an independent U.S. community-based hospital. In early 2015, the organization had been named a top 50 hospital in the United States by a well-known, nationally recognized agency. Success was consistent within the organization throughout its evolution in business model and practice. Health care is a fierce and competitive environment where the independent hospital model is rapidly eroding. This particular organization has consistently faced challenges of remaining as an independent health system when the industry has shifted to purchasing smaller organizations by larger and more complex health care systems. Additional pressures surfaced in the state of this particular organization where certification of public need (COPN) was beginning to be questioned in capitalistic necessity and relevance. Essentially, under COPN, larger health care organizations are prohibited from entering markets without an identified social health care need. A community hospital, without COPN, could be directly threatened by the opening of a larger health system constructing an outpatient (high profit service line) across the street from their facility. Suddenly, local community-based marketing and development can become compromised by lower cost care within the same community. Due to sensitivity and confidentiality factors surrounding the health system, the name of the organization and individuals contributing to the study have been omitted.

In early 2016, this organization was facing declining outpatient elective procedures and significant financial setbacks. To address these setbacks, organizational leadership cut into the heart of its operation without warning. Employees were suddenly informed the annual market adjusted wage increases were suspended, tuition programs were eliminated, and retirement contributions were put on hold with no reinstatement date in sight. All this occurred at the same time that the organization proudly proclaimed that it could operate for nearly 2 years with zero revenue while employing and spending as though the facilities were at full capacity.

Rather than going to the war chest, the organization cut off expenses associated with its own employees. Recruitment was slowed, positions were exceedingly decreased, and several openings began to be eliminated. Financially, in labor and employment, the organization was moving to a forecast-based model where future needs were based on present experience. In such a situation, the forecast model creates a consistent downward trajectory where there is no *correction* of shortage, but rather a steady decline in employment. While inpatient volumes (those demanding consistent staffing) were higher than budgeted, the organization boasted a decrease of more than 200 full-time equivalency (FTE) openings. Many of these decreases in staffing were associated with declined and highly profitable outpatient procedures whereas on the inpatient side decreased staffing directly impacted patient care, safety, and performance.

Case Study Background

Moving into its second decade of success, the health system was facing declining scores in employee and patient satisfaction, significant financial setbacks, and growing management turnover. Based on the time when the case study was conducted, employee satisfaction scores over the prior 5 years are presented in Figure 5.1 to identify characteristics that existed before the cultural disruption and downturn. Employee satisfaction reports were analyzed to explore the positive and negative aspects in areas such as pay, resources, and engagement. Also, interviews with four employees from various operational areas of the organization were conducted and are presented in the following paragraphs alongside patient satisfaction scores during the same period. These scores indicate a significant relationship between employee dissatisfaction and patient

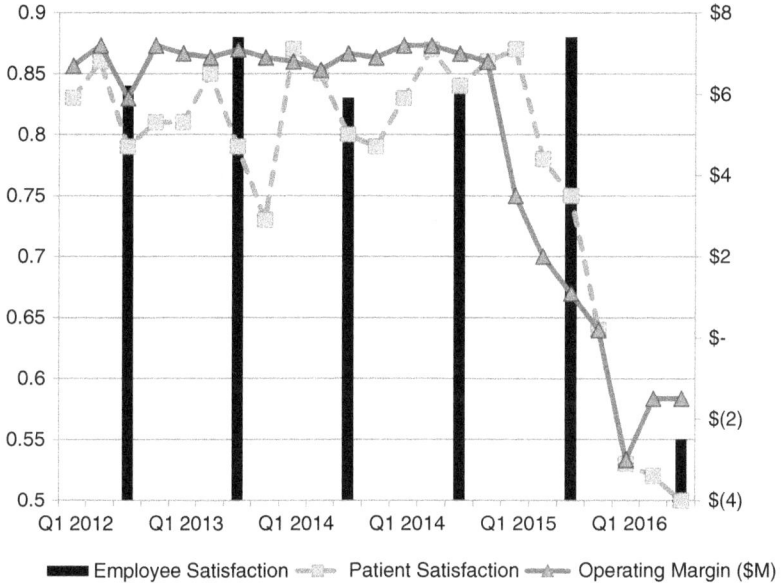

Figure 5.1 Timeline of events in case study factors

dissatisfaction. Management members were interviewed to understand the dynamics within the operational environment through interviews conducted with various employees including an administrative director, nursing director, training and development director, and an employee relation's manager. The interviews sought to understand the most significant challenges and what interviewees felt most greatly contributes to management turnover.

Data Observation—Correlations

Employee satisfaction, patient satisfaction, and financial performance are presented in Figure 5.1. As provided by the employee relations manager, employee satisfaction scores for the past five years were 84 percent (2012), 88 percent (2013), 83 percent (2014), 88 percent (2015) and 55 percent (2016). The historical data prior to 2016 did not have any significant indicators of employee satisfaction or dissatisfaction, though pay was poorly rated in 2014. Employees did, however, receive a fairly significant market-based adjustment in 2015, resulting in a positive adjustment in 2016 for pay responses, though the remaining pillars of the survey included notable declines. The top four concerns in the 2016 survey indicated: (1) strong perception that resources were not sufficient to perform the job expected, (2) the organization failed to act in the best interests of patients, (3) the organization failed to act in the best interests of the employees, and (4) failed to act in the best interests of the community as a community-based health system.

Leadership Interview Results

The information collection process included interviews conducted with four management members within the organization (presented in Table 5.1). First, the employee relations manager shared six key factors; four factors are based on the frontline employee areas, and two are based on the management area. The four employee factors were: (1) workforce reduction, (2) suspension of retirement contributions, (3) closure of clinics, and (4) retraction of raises. The management factors included: (1) excessive delay in fill time for vacancies and (2) nearby competitors were being sought for employment opportunities among the health system and organizational leadership. Essentially, a leader exodus was underway where leaders were suddenly seeking employment with nearby competitors, including university health systems and larger regional health systems.

Table 5.1 Leadership interview results

Interviewee	Management-Level Contributors	Employee-Level Contributors
Employee Relations Manager	70+ day Vacancy Fill Time	Workforce reduction
	Competitors Nearby	Benefit suspension
		Closure of Clinics
		Retraction of Pay Raises
Administrative Director		Days cash on hand
		Productivity imbalance
Training and Development Director	Productivity, department justification	Staffing cuts and development challenges
DON	Best Practices	Development and training
	Time use	Best practices – patient safety

In the second interview, the administrative director expressed the common knowledge that the organization had enough financial reserve to survive for nearly 2 years with absolutely no income. This common knowledge has a significant impact on employee perceptions. The administrative director also expressed a deep concern for the lack of employee care and the reputation the organization was developing. From an operations financial perspective, the administrative director outlined the challenge of reduced outpatient elective procedures. The staff and management in the hospital who cared for admitted patients were suffering the consequences as inpatient settings were largely unaffected by outpatient volumes.

The third interview with the Director of Training and Development presented an argument that department leaders were facing cuts and could not send staff for training and development opportunities. The volume of new employees entering the organization measures the training and development department's productivity. With a reduced incoming workforce, the productivity had resulted in challenges to provide explanations to justify the organizational development department. Fourth, the Director of Nursing (DON) was interviewed for the impact on the staffing cuts and described nursing coverage that is, according to best practices, roughly four patients per nurse (for the specialty of care of the most prominent patient population in the facility). However, nurses were caring for seven to eight patients daily. The DON also expressed that her time at work was largely spent in a nursing role, limiting her management and leadership duties.

Frontline Employee Interview Results

Interviews conducted with four frontline employees, included in Table 5.1, yielded a high amount of emotional frustration, related to eroded motivation, lacking engagement, and an overall strong presence of organizational culture influence on workplace attitudes. It was truly a sad experience to observe such a great organization implode in such a short period of time.

The first interview with a frontline nursing professional resulted in sharing of a mindset that the organization had lost touch with the bedside staff, caregivers, physical therapists, and other professionals. While these career professionals were largely intrinsically motivated by their careers, the environment has shown to be detrimental to the collective employee attitude. This was supported by the interview with a frontline management member who reemphasized the retracted pay adjustment and the suspension of the retirement contribution benefits as shown in Table 5.2. A second frontline employee presented some very powerful feedback illustrating productivity challenges and management frustrations as she worked at both the health system, and a nearby competitor. In the competitor health system, the subject organization of this case study is gaining a reputation that, though the nursing pay is relatively competitive, they are now known to have cut sign-on bonuses and there is no education reimbursement as it has been recently eliminated alongside the suspension of retirement contribution. With this knowledge and existing perceptions in the competitor environment among employees, the issue is clearly large enough within the organization that it has reverberated beyond the organization's own walls and community. Unfortunately, for this organization, more than one dozen equal-sized or larger health care facilities and systems existed within 100 miles of the front door competing for the same patients and employees.

Table 5.2 Employee interview results

Interviewee	Organizational issue contributors
Employee 1	Connection—the organization has lost touch
Employee 2	Promised raises Benefit retraction
Manager 1	Working at both facility and nearby competitor
Manager 2	Clinics employee in regional setting, staff in clinics feel forgotten

To provide insight to the regional settings, the fourth interview, with a regional frontline manager among regional clinics, presented feedback on the regional clinics as seemingly holding the collective feeling that the organization had forgotten the clinics and communities; activities and initiatives in community involvement are largely done independently and without the main hospital support.

Organizational Behavior Observations

Given the analysis of the organizational symptoms of declining patient experience scores, there have been declining employee satisfaction scores, financial setbacks, and management-level turnover. This included organizational challenges which appear to be solely centered on leadership actions in terms of responding to unprecedented challenges in engagement, inclusion, care, concern, or communication. All elements of the organizational leadership response are the root cause of the issues at hand at the employee level. The impact of employee satisfaction with organizational performance correlation is presented in Figure 5.1, distinctively demonstrating the organizational leadership response.

Influence on Motivation

Figure 4.2 outlines intrinsic and extrinsic factors of motivation as outlined by Herzberg (1959). Fundamentally, among other factors, intrinsic factors (achievement, work itself, responsibility) have been adversely influenced by the organizational environment among employees in the health care system. Role achievement and work itself among inpatient nursing professionals was adversely impacted due to workloads exceeding professional practices of safe and quality patient care. Role achievement and work itself motivators are directly influenced by the ability to complete tasks and the work performed contributing to contentment. Next, the responsibility factor, driven by autonomous actions to complete a task was overwhelming. Workplace task autonomy, as a motivation factor, is compromised when workload demands exceed individual ability to complete tasks at a quality level. This is related to the former motivation factors of achievement and the work itself. Responsibility is also significantly related to workload stress, outlined as a direct patient experience feedback correlation later. Lastly, among intrinsic factors, advancement and growth were adversely impacted through positive benefits of employment through role fulfillment and growth opportunity through advancing and supporting educational attainment and skills. Essentially, the elimination of tuition assistance and reduced workforce leaves nursing professionals with little motivation to grow with the current employer. All of this, being based in intrinsic motivation among a profession widely known to be intrinsically motivated leaves very little motivational connection for organizational commitment.

In extrinsic motivation, most factors (company policies, supervision, relationship with supervisor, relationship with peers, working conditions, salary, status, and security) were adversely affected. Policies and organizational leadership clearly eradicate any related motivation, though relationships with direct supervisors may be enhanced in such an environment. Consistently, relationships with peers may be enhanced as workgroups begin to operate in subculture and counterculture behaviors. Inevitably, working conditions, by way of limited nursing resources, adversely impact the extrinsic factor. Salary and job status are largely unaffected apart from increased workloads and monetary compensation. The job security motivation is based on two frames of thought: job security is assumed to be sustained through employment while it is also filled with apprehension through elimination of positions.

Table 5.3 Organizational commitment measures (Celis 2018)

I would be happy to spend the rest of my career with my employer.
Staying with my organization is a matter of necessity as much as desire.
I feel no obligation to remain with my employer.
I feel as though my employer's problems are my own.
It would be hard for me to leave my employer now, even if I wanted to.
Even if it was to my advantage, I do not feel it would be right to leave my employer.
I do not feel a strong sense of belonging to my employer.
Too much of my life would be disrupted if I chose to leave my employer.
I would feel guilty if I left my organization.
I do not feel emotionally attached to my employer.
I feel there are too few alternative employment options to consider leaving my employer.
My employer deserves my loyalty.
I do not feel like a part of a family with my employer.
If I had not already put in so much personal physical and emotional effort into my employer, I might consider working elsewhere.
I would not leave my employer now because I have a sense of obligation to the individuals in it.
My employer has a great deal of personal meaning for me.
One of the few negative consequences of me leaving my employer would be the scarcity of available alternatives.
I owe a great deal to my employer.

Influence on Organizational Commitment

Organizational commitment factors are outlined in Table 5.3. Identifying the specific factor influence on the cultural disruption case study provides an anticipation of results and outcomes. Out of the 18 items (presented as 1 to 18), it is possible to determine a level of influence within the seven point Likert scale design (strongly disagree to strongly agree). Scale measures 1, 4, 9, 10, and 12 are adversely influenced by the cultural disruption. Commitment measures for 2, 5, 6, 11, 14, and 17 are adversely influenced by the cultural breakdown of focus on individuals and their contribution to role performance and achievement. Measures 3, 7, 8, 13, 15, 16, and 18 are based on the individual emotional connection and instinctual needs. As mentioned previously, the subject organization for this case study provides a gap of emotional connectedness among nursing professionals. Further, there are employment opportunities with more favorable benefits for professionals in local communities. Overall, all organizational commitment measures are unsurprisingly adversely affected. There remains little-to-no motivational connection or commitment connectedness to remain with such an organization, apart from subculture and counterculture settings.

CHAPTER 6

Frontline Health Care Employee Motivation and Commitment Study

Human capital is essential to any organization where there is a reliance on human resource (HR) departments to increase competitive employee performance. Strategic HR practices include improving and influencing behaviors and motivation (Truxillo 2015). Organizations depend on the performance of employees to meet goals and succeed.

Tenure of employees relates to attrition and retention; the longer employees remain with an organization, the higher their willingness to continue with the same employer (Jena et al. 2017). Employee tenure becomes a predictor of organizational commitment that can change depending on motivation factors (e.g., employee engagement, job satisfaction, and meaningful work; Jena et al. 2017). As previously outlined, organizations compete, domestically and internationally, for talented employees in a global marketplace presenting daily career opportunities that entice workers to move to different employers (Bala 2016). Targeted recruitment becomes critical, demanding employers to motivate, retain, and develop employees with greater levels of focus and results, as opposed to commonly accepting turnover as an industry standard or phenomenon (Bala 2016). Thus, motivation influences employee commitment, driving organizational performance.

Organizations invest considerable financial and human capital resources into reward systems to motivate employees to maximize organizational effectiveness and success (Antoni et al. 2017). Motivation has been described as a behavioral force driving employee performance, affecting organizational effectiveness (McShane et al. 2009). Organizations analyze factors of employee motivation, behavior, and performance to determine, strategize, and enhance new ways to motivate their workforce. Motivated employees exert greater levels of effort, time, and persistence to meet organizational goals.

Purpose of the Study on Health Care Service Workers

The purpose of the health care service worker study was to investigate the relationship between employee motivation factors and affective organizational commitment in private sector service workers in a health care environment. Increasing understanding of what factors contribute to employee motivation and organizational commitment helps organizations foster these key contributors to organizational success. This quantitative correlational study provided evidence regarding the influence of employee motivation factors on affective organizational commitment. The results of this study provide: (1) identification of influential motivation factors for the sample, supporting organizations' abilities to better understand motivations of their workforce and improve organizational effectiveness; (2) assistance in developing employee motivation strategies and improving employee performance by identifying significant factors; and (3) knowledge of motivation factors within the workplace that improves affective organizational commitment.

The study was based on the paucity of research on the relationship between motivational factors and affective organizational commitment in private sector service workers. Past studies on the relationship between motivation and commitment has focused on employees in high-level and professional jobs such as executive leadership positions (Denison and Mishra 1995), skilled health care professionals (Hunt et al. 2012; Tosun and Ulusoy 2017; Williams and Glisson 2014), and engineering and financial professionals (Adair 2011). Professional and highly skilled positions have higher intrinsic motivation, typically due to educational attainment, expertise motivation, and subsequent job fulfillment (Tosun and Ulusoy 2017). Conversely, low-skilled positions are prone to higher levels of extrinsic motivation (e.g., pay and working conditions; Turner 2017). This study focused on low-skilled service workers to determine the need for different motivation systems to maximize the organizational commitment of this population.

The Significance of Examining Motivation and Commitment Factors

The era of globalization forces organizations to be efficient in producing value-added outputs. Efficiency and competitiveness are attainable if organizations employ people with the proper attitudes and skills. Organizations battle for workforce shares in the same way they compete for market shares. Commitment influences employee behaviors and organizational adaptability, including turnover, turnover intentions, attendance, and tardiness rates. Employees with higher levels of commitment are more productive, particularly those with affective organizational commitment through the emotional connection an employee holds with his or her employer. Affective organizational commitment significantly affects organizational climate and structure, leading employees to carry out role requirements in a dependable, engaged fashion with innovation and performance beyond job expectations. Organizational commitment contributes to organizational success through emotional connections (e.g., values of loyalty or a sense of duty) that motivate employees to meet organizational goals (Valeau et al. 2016).

Motivation factors in the workplace shape perceptions and attitudes, reflecting whether employees feel connected to their environment (Cesario et al. 2017). Motivation requires understanding about what makes a good workplace, how employees trust peers and the company, why they have pride in their roles, and intrinsic factors that enhance organizational commitment. When employees work in organizations with shared values and goals, they are more likely to adopt positive behaviors that are consistent with the mission, values, and objectives of the organization and they also develop strong commitment to the organization. Organizational commitment and workplace motivators are critical predictors of organizational effectiveness that promote individual and team achievement, performance, wellbeing, and intentions to stay (Cesario et al. 2017). Employee commitment elevates employee performance and the success of the organization. Conversely, affective organizational commitment can mediate satisfaction with workplace benefits, stay intention, and job satisfaction. Motivation supports organizational commitment while affective organizational commitment supports satisfaction in the workplace to attract, retain, and motivate employees.

Competition for talented employees is a global challenge. Motivation depends on employees' perceptions and attitudes of their employer; the relationship between motivation, perception, and attitude influences organizational commitment (Rafael et al. 2017). Motivation, and the extent to which an employee identifies with an organization, mediates organizational commitment where intrinsic and extrinsic motivation factors influence organizational commitment (Dinc 2017). With lower levels of motivation, organizational commitment is weaker and organizational commitment declines. Developing an understanding of individual and organizational performance requires understanding the influence of organizational commitment and how to improve it. Recall the services company with a turnover rate exceeding 13 employees per day, as well as the health care organization that met with a disastrous employee relations and operations problem. Understanding the motivation factors of the service workers case study and applying appropriate strategies to counterbalance motivations, such as what is considered to be a positive workplace, may have been employed to improve retention. For the health care organization, had the senior leaders been more in tune with employee perceptions and motivation factors, the impact on employee engagement, operating revenue, and patient experience may have been lessened. When you attach dollars, productivity, and organizational performance to motivation and commitment, it becomes quite logical that it is a critical opportunity for organizations to improve on many levels.

Herzberg's theory of work motivation was ideal for this study through its consistency in findings among contemporary research studies related to motivation and organizational commitment. Herzberg's (1959) model proposes three interactions between intrinsic and extrinsic factors in the response of individuals to multiple stimuli and postulates that both intrinsic and extrinsic motivation factors are necessary to describe workplace satisfaction (Vijayakumar and Saxena 2015). First, intrinsic factors include recognition, achievement, growth, advancement, and job fulfillment. Second, extrinsic factors include salary, interpersonal relations, supervision, working conditions, and job security. Lastly, job satisfaction and dissatisfaction are orthogonal dimensions that influence satisfaction motivated by factors other than dissatisfaction. Essentially, organizations must address one set of factors to increase job satisfaction and another to reduce job dissatisfaction (Vijayakumar and Saxena 2015).

Research Question and Hypotheses of the Health Care Service Worker Study

Research Question

RQ: Are workplace motivator factors correlated with affective organizational commitment of service workers in a health care environment?

Data Examination and Results of the Health Care Service Worker Study

The study evaluated motivation factors and their influence on affective organizational commitment among service workers in a health care environment. To maintain anonymity of participants, all the data from each location was summarized as one dataset before beginning the analysis. Data examination was inclusive of responses from selected health care support services departments participating in the study agreeing to participate after reviewing the letter of informed consent.

Sample Characteristics

This study included participants from multiple sites who were service workers in a health care environment. The study was executed through paper and electronic survey collection. The overall response rate for paper surveys was 90 percent. The response rate was 67 percent for surveys completed via an online link. Most participants were 30 to 39 years old (30.5 percent); 73.3 percent were female and 22.9 percent male with an average length of experience of 4.9 years in their current position. All participants worked in service worker positions; no participants held management roles of any capacity.

Hypotheses and Results

The correlations between independent variables and motivation were tested with Pearson's correlations. Results indicated support for affective commitment, normative commitment, and overall commitment. Continuance commitment showed no correlation with motivation factors. Pearson's correlation analysis identified four distinct outcomes (see Table 5.1). First, there was a significant correlation between affective commitment and motivation; $r = .38$, $p < .001$. As affective commitment increased, motivation increased. Consequently, the alternative hypothesis predicting that workplace motivation factors are correlated with affective

Table 6.1 Comparison of studies examining motivation factor rank (most to least)

Question	S1	S2 (Fareed and Jan 2016)	S3 (Ozturk et al. 2016)	S4 (Hunt et al. 2012)
Use of abilities	1			
Job security	2	4	2	
Coworker relations	3	3		
Nature of work	4	9		
Supervisor relations	5			
Supervisor knowledge	6	7		
Achievement motivation	7	6		
Increased responsibilities	8	1		
Policies	9	10		
Quality and accessibility of equipment/tools	10			
Growth	11	2	3	4
Team/group cohesion	12	5		
Advancement/ promotion	13	11	1	
Recognition	14	8		
Challenging work	15			2
Wages/increases	16	12		3
Work–life balance	17			5
Benefits	18			1

commitment was supported. Second, there was no significant correlation between continuance commitment and motivation; $r = .09, p < 0.35$. Third, there was a significant correlation between normative commitment and motivation; $r = .38, p < .001$. As normative commitment increased, motivation increased. Lastly, there was significant correlation between overall organizational commitment and motivation; $r = .35, p < .001$. As organizational commitment increased, motivation increased. Collectively, the results of this study address the research question of whether workplace motivation factors are correlated with affective organizational commitment, including the overall organizational commitment analysis.

Summary of the Study

The purpose of the health care service worker study was to investigate the relationship between employee motivation factors and affective organizational commitment among private sector service workers in a health care environment (technicians). Existing research in the fields of workplace motivation and organizational commitment identified private sector service workers as an underrepresented group. A quantitative approach of regression was utilized to analyze the correlation between workplace motivation factors and identified motivation factors as significantly correlated with affective organizational commitment among service workers in a health care environment. The study identified the relationship between motivation and commitment among service workers to provide a foundation for organizations to: identify influential motivation factors associated with commitment; develop motivation strategies to improve employee performance; and understand motivation factors within the workplace that improve affective organizational commitment.

Results and Study Comparisons

One of the most significant drivers behind this study is based in the substantial absence of service worker observations on motivation and commitment. Many studies, as have been outlined previously, exist in measuring motivation and commitment among professional and high-skill roles and positions. Utilizing the service worker approach provides a glimpse into employee groups with lower education requirements, lower training requirements, and a much lower requirement for specific technological skill. Service workers are those in support services roles, including linen health care services. However, the service worker population, in an environment of high levels of professional skills, education, and training is uniquely qualified to investigate motivation and commitment in the same way the two constructs have been examined in the same environment with more specialized roles. Table 6.1 illustrates the variance in motivation factors across various workgroups. Results indicate high skill levels within health care are similarly motivated by job security while other leading factors appear to be inverse of those most important to service worker roles. However, motivation factors in a banking organization show similarities in job security, peer relations, supervisor knowledge, achievement, workplace policies, and advancement.

CHAPTER 7

Shifts in Health Care Culture and Delivery of Care

The evolution of health care has led to a shift in focus from the delivery of patient care and organizational change through development of cultures (Anders and Cassidy 2014). This has been motivated by the demand for health care organizations to competitively operate. The evolving patient population in terms of age, mental health needs, and other chronic illnesses, along with the rising costs associated with health care, led to the shift towards delivering care though a patient-oriented approach (Anders and Cassidy 2014). Though the shift in care delivery for health care organizations is encouraged by industry change, it is difficult for health care organizations to easily adjust to health care reform. Competitive strategies include value-based care where patients are increasingly viewed as the most important individuals participating in the delivery of care (Anders and Cassidy 2014).

From a clinical perspective, clinical outcomes have shown to be improved when patients are included in their care process and feel their voices and concerns are heard (Anders and Cassidy 2014). Considering other dimensions of competitiveness, patients now have significant power in both the competition and the financial rewards of health care organizations (McClelland and Vogus 2014). In 2013, the Center for Medicaid Services (CMS) implemented a pay-for-performance and value-based model that allows hospitals to earn back reimbursement funds withheld by Medicare and Medicaid as a financial reward for clinical outcomes, patient feedback, mortality, and additional performance measures. The reimbursements and competitive components are driven by government implementation of the Hospital Consumer Assessment of Healthcare Providers and Systems (HCAHPS) survey where patients provide feedback on experience, satisfaction, and overall facility rankings.

Shifting to a patient-oriented culture requires a tenacious and committed workforce for effective change that focuses on the development of high-quality workplace environments with the associated staff satisfaction and quality in care delivery (Brunoro-Kadash and Kadash 2013). While many health care organizations continue to hold strong to operating with a focus on capacity and bed planning, the focus on patient bedside care time as a factor of patient-centered care has been identified as an influence on both patient and employee satisfaction through the emphasis on efficiency. However, the outcomes mentioned in the foregoing text point to a collective level of satisfaction in the development of efficiency and high-quality work environments as it relates to nursing staff, patients, and all employees with the organization. While satisfaction alignment remains as an important indicator, the focus on the cultural development factors precedes the outcome.

Health Care Organizational Change

With the implementation of patient advocacy and liaison representation within health care systems, the focus on patient empowerment has continued to grow as patient-centered care has become more of a reality than ever before. As an orienting purpose, the collection of staff, patient, and public involvement during the course of care has placed demands on the delivery of care shift and the need to provide sufficient resources and leadership to guide change management. Consequently, through the demands and change, patient engagement has emerged as a core focus as a result of policy and reform changes in the industry. Such liaison and advocacy groups seek to drive organizational change to deliver care that collaborates with patients in the care they receive with a voice. The emerging practice supports allowing patients to have an influence in the treatment they receive. Liaison groups declare a vision of ensuring patient and family voices are valued via shared decision making for each patient. This approach provides empowerment for patients by providing the opportunity to share active feedback and voicing of concerns, leading to stronger patient-centered care (Brunoro-Kadash and Kadash 2013).

Compassionate Practice and Patient Perceptions

To connect the compassionate practices and cultures with patient perceptions, high levels of compassionate practice, measured as the extent of compassionate acts supporting both employees and patients, has indicated positive outcomes and strong correlations with facility ratings and recommendations (McClelland and Vogus 2014). As previously mentioned, the CMS implementation of HCAHPS has provided financial and competitive incentives for organizations to focus on patient-centered care that is improved when organizations and care staff focus on empathy in needs, preferences, and responsiveness to patients. Further, the compassionate care and behavior perspectives focus on treating the whole patient, rather than only the illness, that produces more favorable patient experiences in terms of satisfaction and quality. Outcomes of compassionate care resulted in improvement of overall facility ranking and clinical outcomes with reduced readmission rates through the improvement in perceived quality of care simply through behavioral aspects and patient medical adherence (McClelland and Vogus 2014).

Health Care Culture and Subcultures

Consistent with industry evolution, health care organizations exist in an industry of constant change that previously allowed health care facilities to operate in conditions less driven by the typical laws of supply and demand through facility-specific insurance coverage (Bellou 2008). During this time of evolution, public competitive measures identified were absent; essentially, the health care industry has evolved into an environment of fierce competition. The focus on patient-centered care results in challenges for survival and pressure to reduce the costs of health care with the demands driven by consumer preference. However, in patient-centered care, the focus is to improve patients' experiences through changing the behavior and culture within the health care environment while maintaining processes that internally drive the functions associated with patient care (Bellou 2008).

Moving into organizational change, a cultural environment must be developed to alter and form employee priorities, behaviors, and attitudes so that beliefs and values are shared across organizational members.

However, one of the most significant issues with changing cultures is that many employees are recruited from other health systems and may have established norms, standards, values, and expectations that are not aligned with their current environment. Within the health care environment of other systems and providers, service quality ultimately drives consumer preferences within an environment of growing customer loyalty and perceived higher levels of service quality (Bellou 2008). As a result, all frontline staff in patient and non-patient care roles must cooperate to provide the highest level of patient care in terms of patient perceptions.

Evolving Patient Expectations

Also, consistent with contemporary research indicating industry evolution, the significance of growing expectations in compassionate care should be acknowledged by health care organizations, clinical staff, and physicians. The shift from physician-oriented care delivery to patient-oriented care has higher demands including communication, consideration of feelings of patients, grasping patient thoughts, perceptions, and understanding (Choi et al. 2015). The passive patient role in receiving care and, thus, gaining an understanding to patient expectations is important for implementing an environment of patient-focused care where care providers and patients share information and power in the care process, known as *care sharing* (Choi et al. 2015). The expanding availability of medical information online and various additional forms of media allow patients to have more insight into different opinions regarding the treatment of diagnosed illnesses (Choi et al. 2015). Additionally, patients are increasingly selecting their health care services based on customer service-oriented factors. Lastly, from the financial perspective over prior years, patients are spending more of their individual income on health care due to rising patient age (Choi et al. 2015). Collectively, the evolving trends for care sharing has proven to be a positive practice for implementing patient-centered care in clinical environments.

Evidence-based outcomes associated with patient feedback and satisfaction show improved medical, physical, and psychological outcomes are more likely when providers have a balanced level of trust and respect for patients (Choi et al. 2015). It is important to note the shared decision-making approach to care is subject to demographic factors, including mental health, age, nationality, language, and education level. Strategies should be developed around patient knowledge and agreement so that treatment may be more successful when patients have less conflict in personal values, beliefs, lifestyles, and other aspects unique to various patient populations.

Nursing Subculture and Patient Outcomes

An additional dimension to assessing the effectiveness of compassionate practices, patient satisfaction, and clinical outcomes that must be considered is the role of subcultures in health care. Subculture presence in all organizations may be associated with organizational performance, such as clinical outcomes in patient care within subculture care groups (Mallidou et al. 2010). The consideration of subcultures is based on sublevel differentiation within the organization where groups become high-functioning in performance and behaviors. Further, the cultural need for change, in contrast to the influence of subcultures, demonstrates the associated benefits and outcomes.

Subculture groups are also able to react more nimbly than the organization as a whole when responding to change and embracing innovative practices through higher levels of communication and acceptance to individual differences (Mallidou et al. 2010). Outcomes in clinical settings associated with higher levels of subculture richness improves the quality of patient care and patient safety through collective group skills in maintaining desired outcomes through identification, development, describing, and collaborating for the delivery of care (Mallidou et al. 2010). This association between culture and behavioral factors is consistent with previously identified literature by identifying behaviors as they relate to patient outcomes and satisfaction.

Developing Cultures of Compassion in Care Delivery

Developing a culture of supportive care provides patient-centered focus as patients desire to be treated with respect, dignity, and emotional support. Patients are increasingly interested in receiving complete information regarding the care they are receiving (Richardson 2004). Though a culture of support provides a foundation for improved patient experiences and outcomes, there are limitations that may be present during the course of care. Of many limitations, the most significant limitations include recognizing patient need without meeting those needs; caregivers fail to utilize relevant resources; or lack of communication to deliver the maximum impact on the care provided (Richardson 2004).

Given the patient preferences and shortfalls of a culture of supportive care, there are multiple strategies to develop and sustain a culture of supportive care. First, on a foundational level, a culture of consistent patient focus must be developed where caregivers consistently assess patient treatment (Richardson 2004). Second, teams must work to integrate care through effective teamwork in valuing patients and improving focus through evidence and needs underpinning the delivery of care (Richardson 2004). The third strategy is having teams that work together without fear or influence of other groups of professionals while sharing values, decision making, and responsibilities (Richardson 2004). Lastly, cultural should emphasize collaboration, diversity, shared planning, and relationships that are not based on hierarchical characteristics (Richardson 2004). These collective factors can improve the delivery of patient care by improving culture via patient feedback, clinical outcomes, and competitive factors associated with financial and operational performance.

Enablers and Barriers to Delivering Compassionate Care

Cultural perspectives, organizational change, patient expectations, and perceptions have been explored. An additional critical aspect in creating an environment of compassionate care is to analyze enabler and barriers in health care environments in the delivery of compassionate care. Growing concerns in the lack of compassionate care practices has led to recommendations from authoritative nursing councils and associations to evaluate the factors affecting nursing practices (Christiansen et al. 2014). A commonly developed theme has surfaced in the focus on cultural values underpinning a culture of compassionate care, including care provided, commitment, communication, courage, empathy, and competence.

From a definitive perspective, compassionate care may be described as the acknowledgement of caregivers in the human response to the vulnerabilities and needs of others (Christiansen et al. 2014). This awareness and acknowledgement builds interpersonal interactions and relationships that are based on how people relate to one another.

In identifying the enablers and barriers to the delivery of compassionate care, three dimensions are explored: individual factors, organizational factors, and leadership and team factors (Christiansen et al. 2014). Regarding individual factors, enablers are commonly identified as values one holds personally and professionally, as well as attributes of approachability and lacking judgement on others. Barriers compromising compassionate care on the individual level largely reveal workload-related factors, including long working shifts, fatigue, not receiving breaks from work, and hunger (Christiansen et al. 2014). Organizational factors compromising the delivery of compassionate care revealed workload volumes, limited time to spend with patients, shortages in staffing, and the perceptions of the business approach to health care in focusing less on patient care and more on operational efficiency and costs (Christiansen et al. 2014). In leadership and team factors, enabling characteristics included a culture of leadership support, collaborative and supportive behaviors among teams, and role models for compassionate care (Christiansen et al. 2014).

CHAPTER 8

The Study on Bedside Engagement and Patient Experience Feedback

Patient experience measures and feedback have reached the forefront of health care organizational strategy since the 2008 implementation of the Healthcare Consumer Assessment of Healthcare Providers and Systems (HCAHPS) survey (HCAHPS Online n.d.). The government-administered survey from CMS is driven to provide financial incentives for quality and experience performance while also providing transparent consumer reporting and quality of care improvement (HCAHPS Online n.d.). To meet the emerging focus on improving patient experience, health care organizations are adopting the ideology and practices of patient-centered care as a critical approach to meet patient challenges. To expand upon the shift in focus and strategy, patient experience and outcomes are influenced not only by liaison and patient-centered practices, but also by characteristics and behaviors in the work environment. Consequently, these characteristics affect care quality associated with injuries, falls, overall outcomes, and patient experiences and perceptions (Hahtela et al. 2017).

The study on workplace engagement among bedside health care employees and patient experience observations explores the patient experience aspects in the delivery of care by combining cultural aspects within the health care environment. While contemporary research explores patient experience, quality of care, and clinical outcomes, there is little research regarding cultural factors associated with patient feedback on cultural behaviors. This study identified what specific organizational culture behaviors are significantly associated with patient experience feedback outcomes. The study on workplace engagement and patient experience also investigated measures for cultural behaviors and factors in the health care environment from the employee perception perspective. Lastly, this identified how employee perceptions and engagement correlate with patient experience feedback in specific questions from the HCAHPS survey associated with specific questions and domains for culturally driven employee behaviors.

Purpose of the Study

The purpose of this health care study was to examine the relationship between indicators of what health care organizational measures are culturally and behaviorally present compared to patients' observations regarding nurses' behaviors. The goal of the study was to identify the correlation between indicators of employee levels of cultural factors and the patient experience feedback in the same settings. Research regarding the central topic of health care organizational culture has uncovered that patient experience feedback is significantly related to organizational culture. However, little research exists on examining the relationship between health care organization cultural measures and patients' perceptions of the culture and behavior of nurses. Essentially, contemporary observations suggest that health care organizations apply cultural strategies on a largely consistent basis across the industry. However, the behavioral components driving culture and strategy associated with patient experience feedback do not always translate to the patient experience. The problem associated with health care culture and patient experience feedback is based on the strategic approach to improve feedback. From this perspective, there is little insight between understanding perceived cultural presence, engagement among health care employees, and the cultural richness perceived from patients in feedback performance scores.

Patient experience is driven by perceptions of care based on both compassionate practices and quality of care received. Current observations conclude behavioral practices among employees to be the link for success, while lacking in the connection is how to evaluate and measure behavior in the environment as it relates to strategy and practice for improving patient satisfaction. Regarding cultural and behavioral development in the organization, present research points to the need to strategically develop cultures aimed at improving patient experience performance. Frameworks must be established, including the development of a culture to support patient experiences in communications, transparency, engagement, and empathetic environments (Birkelien 2017).

Though patient perceptions and cultural need may be viewed as key factors in the health care environment, it is more critical to understand what cultural behaviors are associated with patient experience feedback and how to evaluate the presence, or "richness," of those characteristics. By evaluating the level of cultural richness through correlations with patient experience performance, an assessment may be made and utilized to determine the impact of perceived cultural behaviors on patient satisfaction performance. The study is structured around the evaluation of employee perceptions of cultural factors in 11 hospitals in the upper Midwest, including community, academic, and acute care hospitals.

Ultimately, this health care employee and patient experience feedback study sought to understand the relationship between perceived cultural presence and patient experience feedback by utilizing the HCAHPS survey for 2017.

Premise of the Study

In both theory and application, health care organizations should identify a means to connect cultural initiatives and strategies with patient experience outcomes. Historically, there has been a growing focus on cultural development within health care organizational settings, though the focus is rarely correlated or measured against patient experience feedback. The cultural strategy aspect is evidenced in the approach in competitive advantage and patient focus. For hospitals to maintain competitive advantages, a framework must be established that includes the development of a culture to support patient experiences, facilitating patient communications, information transparency, patient engagement, organization accessibility to customers, and development of empathy (Birkelien 2017). This is emphasized through understanding patients as unique individuals, grasping thoughts and emotions of the patient, and communicating with a concept of caring while establishing a relationship that shares information and decisions between providers and patients (Choi et al. 2015).

Outside the specific health care setting, organizational culture literature contains significant opportunities in identifying perceived culture among employees, though organizational operating culture continues to be a significant driver of organizational strategy. Thus, the problem of connecting culture to outcomes is further met with the opportunity of connecting culture to frontline perception among health care employees with the subsequent correlation to patient feedback. Perceived culture is an essential key to the connection whereby links in the relationship between motivation, productivity, and authentic behaviors hold further positive consequences on psychological well-being (Reis et al. 2016). With organizational culture influencing how one believes he or she should behave, different cultures create different environments providing insight to employees about the extent to which one may feel safe in behaving authentically. The connection to authentic behaviors is significant as authenticity influences engagement, motivation, and fulfillment while stimulating employee behavior to work in activities that fit core values more consistently with their core selves (Reis et al. 2016). With cultural aspects, it is important to understand and develop cultural awareness in attitudes, skills, and knowledge regarding patients and coworkers (Lateef 2017). Though the culture factor is a common strategic practice in most health care organizations presently, few are able to attain the desired patient experience feedback measures.

Patient Experience

Patient experience is evaluated in terms of existing and emerging practices as those practices that are related to cultural development. As a concept and focus in practice, patient experience is a relatively new term and objective in the health care industry from the strategic cultural development perspective. Patient experience and culture is viewed as the key for improvement in understanding the correlation between culture and patient satisfaction (Pilav and Jatic 2017). Patient experience is driven by cultural structure in power and typology in both external and internal aspects composed of patterns of shared assumptions within the organization. With this framework, patient experience has consequently shown significant levels of growth in bringing patients and families into the center of the delivery of care (Ryan 2017). As patient experience becomes a cornerstone in developing cultures seeking to understand patient perspectives, factors driving patient experience and employee culture include training, daily huddles, recognition, and modeling practices, which are becoming commonplace.

Research Method

The research method was based on an observational study through a survey design. The surveys utilized are gathered from third-party vendors, CMS (through Press Ganey) and Willis Towers Watson. From the foundation of the research study, and the approach of a quantitative method, the cross-sectional design was employed. Relationships among patient satisfaction measures and employee perceived cultural measures were examined in a specific period of time. The cross-sectional design allows for observation of the patient population and the employee population data in the survey method approach. Essentially, results are derived from the relationships among each population within defined measures and factors for analysis, and, most importantly, simultaneous time periods.

The population for the observation in this study includes patients and employees within an upper Midwest metropolitan area. The patient population is based on acute care patients discharged from 11 area hospitals between January 1, 2017 and December 31, 2017. Consistently, employee samples are based on employees surveyed in employee engagement surveys between January 1, 2017 and December 31, 2017.

For the patient population of this research study, the sample was appropriate as the individuals within the sample have all completed the same standardized HCAHPS survey and can be observed in terms of the relationships with the employee population perceptions of engagement. Additionally, the 11 hospitals utilized in the population include academic, inner city, community, and rural critical access hospitals. In other words, all patients were admitted to the hospital and were in acute care settings, excluding mental health and pediatric patients, within the same window of time. To further underscore the value of this population, the data gathered from patient feedback can be separated and analyzed down to the specific unit level at each hospital, providing the opportunity to compare cultures across the sample and patient feedback in like-unit settings.

While HCAHPS data is publicly reported, in order to gather the more specific data, approval from the health system was provided to dissect survey data down to specific questions. The patient sample group, through the data gathered, is anonymous in identity and no individual contact or interventions occurred. Sampling occurred through collecting HCAHPS reports from the third-party survey administrator, Press Ganey, indicating results of each question of the survey. It should further be noted that Press Ganey is the survey administrator for all 11 hospitals.

Employee Population

The employee population for this study is comprised of nearly 13,000 employees within the same 11 hospitals as the patient populations working in bedside care roles, namely, registered nurses (RNs) and licensed practical nurses (LPNs). Definitive demographics are speculative and would be merely based on assumptions, as the sampling method does not provide specific employee demographics. However, analyses suggest 9.1 percent of RNs and 7.6 percent of LPNs as male; average age of LPNs was 43.6 years and 44.6 years for RNs; 75.4 percent are self-identified as Caucasian (Minority Nurse 2015).

The employee population was most suitable for this study as the purpose of the study is to measure the relationship between employee perceived culture and patient feedback. When assessing the relationship between an employee's perceived culture, patient feedback, and the delivery of care, bedside care employees are those who directly interact with the patient. Using the cultural factors of this population of employees identifies the direct relationship in engagement and culture perceived among employees and the behavioral feedback outcomes of patients. The sampling of the employee population, provided by the organization, was extracted through a third-party employee engagement survey analyzing employee satisfaction, cultural measures, and organizational behavior measures as executed in three randomized waves throughout 2017 to ultimately target all employees. Through selection of specific questions within the survey, a model can be developed to create a cultural measure on the whole collective level, as well as site and unit level. In order to utilize this information, approval was provided from the health system organizational learning and development department.

Instrumentation

Instrument #1: Patient Experience Measures—
The HCAHPS Survey

The patient population survey is administered by CMS as the HCAHPS survey through Press Ganey, the third-party administering organization. The survey is based on random patient selection within the qualifiers previously outlined. Overall, the standardized survey contains 26 core questions. Though health care facilities may elect to select additional questions, the 26-question survey is the standardized approach utilized, as it is consistent among all 11 hospitals as an instrument. The instrument, as provided by HCAHPS Online via CMS is provided in Appendix B. The survey is provided in multiple modes, including mail and telephone key entry and is divided into domains that include global ratings (hospital and recommendation ratings), communication with nurses, responsiveness of hospital staff, communication with doctors, hospital environment, communication about pain, pain management, communication about medications, discharge information, care transitions, and personal demographic identifiers. Scaled questions are based on frequency, measured by *always*, *usually*, *sometimes*, and *never*, while ratings questions are based on a Likert 0 to 10 scale.

Due to the identified factors in the delivery of care, communications, pain management, patient-centered care, and cultural perceptions among patients, the following two domains within the HCAHPS survey have been selected for analysis:

- Care from Nurses Domain
- Overall Hospital Rating

Within these two domains exist the critical questions associated with patient care and cultural factors that are provided in Appendix B. Within the Care from Nurses domain, the following questions are utilized to provide a single overall measure:

- *During this hospital stay, how often did nurses treat you with courtesy and respect?*
- *During this hospital stay, how often did nurses listen carefully to you?*
- *During this hospital stay, how often did nurses explain things in a way that you could understand?*
- *During this hospital stay, after you pressed the call button, how often did you get help as soon as you wanted it?*

Additionally, the Overall Hospital Rating domain is utilized for assessment of patient experience feedback. The overall rating question is posed as:

- *Overall rating using any number from 0 to 10, where 0 is the worst hospital possible and 10 is the best hospital possible, what number would you use to rate this hospital during your stay?*

HCAHPS Instrument Components and Rationale

The HCAHPS survey is a standardized approach that nearly all hospitals use as a tool to assess patient experience and to gather feedback, driving accountability for quality improvement, standardization, and experiences. Specific domains have been selected due to the focus on bedside care staff and research factors identified as most significant to patients. In this approach, compassionate practices are correlated with indicators of perceptions on care quality and feedback through measures; most specifically, the overall hospital rating. Patients want to be heard and treated as individual people involved in the delivery and receipt of care and is evaluated through the communications and listening aspect of the HCAHPS survey factors included in the analysis. The selection of these questions further represents patient-centered care where compassion, listening, attentiveness, and consideration are central to patient preferences.

Instrument #2: Willis Towers Watson Employee Engagement Survey

The employee population survey is administered by the selected health system across all 11 hospitals in the sample. The survey is composed of 34 questions with dimensions of employee commitment, leadership perceptions, line of sight, sustainable engagement, teamwork, well-being, and work environment. The instrument is provided in Appendix C.

Within the employee culture assessment and measures, the following two measures are utilized:

- Sustainable Engagement
- Employee Commitment

Within Sustainable Engagement, as outlined in Appendix C, the following statements are addressed:

- *I am proud to work for or be affiliated with this organization;*
- *There are no substantial barriers at work to doing my job well;*
- *I feel valued as an individual in this organization;*
- *I have a good understanding of how my job contributes to this organization achieving its mission, vision, and strategic plan;*
- *I am able to sustain the level of energy I need throughout the work day;*
- *The organization provides the resources necessary for me to work effectively;*
- *My work group operates effectively as a team;*
- *The stress levels at work are usually manageable;*
- *I would recommend this organization to others as a good place to work.*

Within the Employee Commitment domain, outlined in Appendix B, the following statements are included:

- *I would prefer to remain with this organization, even if a comparable job were available in another organization;*
- *I am proud to work for or be affiliated with this organization;*
- *I would recommend this organization to others as a good place to work;*
- *Overall, how satisfied are you with this organization at the present time.*

This instrument was administered to organization employees in three randomized waves in March 2017, June 2017, and September 2017. One key observation of the organization is the focus on continual employee engagement and cultural focus. Rather than doing a single full survey annually, the waves maintain a focus throughout each year.

Willis Towers Watson Instrument Components and Rationale

The use of the employee engagement survey provides multiple measures within the two dimensions utilized. First, cultural variables may be assessed from evaluating performance, quality, and, most importantly, engagement. This is consistent with the sustainable engagement dimension utilized in the employee instrument. Second, teamwork and cross-departmental cohesion come into play with evaluating culture, including shared values, beliefs, and assumptions shared within a common group. The questions comprising the sustainable engagement dimension are highly valuable in assessing additional cultural factors for consideration. Health care culture may also be assessed further through psychology, communication, innovation, leadership, and attitudes associated with change (Scott et al. 2003). These factors are included in the employee commitment domain. Lastly, employee behavior and culture may be connected through evaluating engagement, motivation, fulfillment, and employee state of mind that supports emotional feelings driving engagement in activities (Reis et al. 2016).

Results

The results of the employee engagement study were mixed across several domains. Overall, the study analyzed 9,766 patient responses and 12,595 RN and LPN responses. Through comparison of hospitals with the overall organization, the majority of hospitals were significantly correlated with the overall organization. The significant correlation suggests overall organizational culture development may be viewed as strongly present in the organization across the enterprise. The overall correlations resulted in an R^2 of 0.993. The parent health system, in consideration of the newly acquired, smaller, health system, held a correlation of 0.978. However, included hospitals represented less than 6 percent of the overall organization and indicated no positive correlation with the parent organization in commitment and sustainable engagement, including all hospitals of the recently purchased and acquired new health system.

For the analysis of employee engagement, commitment and sustainable feedback was assessed. Correlations within the commitment domain indicated preference to remain with an organization was not associated with commitment while having a sense of pride was only marginally supportive of organizational commitment. While these two measures indicate a lacking correlation with commitment, these measures indicate preference to remain with an organization and organizational pride should be evaluated as measures for commitment, as covered in Chapter 3. The analysis of the sustainable engagement domain indicated significant opportunities in developing a sense of understanding of the domain. The statements, "I am able to sustain the level of energy I need through the day," "My work group operates effectively as a team," "I have a good understanding of how my job contributes to this organization achieving its mission, vision, and strategic plan," and "The stress levels at work are usually manageable," indicate a weak correlation with sustainable engagement as an overall measure. However, the statements, "There are no sustainable obstacles at work to doing my job well," "This organization provides the resources necessary for me to work effectively," and "I am proud to work for or to be affiliated with this organization," all had positive correlations with sustainable engagement measures. The significance in organizational measures indicates employee comprehension of job contribution to organization success and stress levels demand cultural development attention.

In analysis across employee engagement domains, organizational pride and recommending the organization as a good place to work significantly correlated with organizational commitment, though in a separately measured domain. The measure of, "I would prefer to remain with this organization…" was negatively correlated with sustainable engagement while overall organizational satisfaction supported sustainable engagement. An observation in the analyses identified the organizational commitment domain to be improved by developing organizational pride and recommendation of the organization as an employer. The sustainable engagement domain may be improved by improving organizational pride.

In analysis of employee engagement and behavior-related patient experience feedback questions, correlations and relationships were somewhat limited. Recommendation of the employer was positively correlated with measures of overall hospital rating with patients receiving call button help as soon as wanted, and nurses listening carefully to patients. Overall satisfaction with the employer was strongly correlated with overall hospital rating, as was the overall commitment domain. The employee engagement statement, "There are no substantial obstacles at work to doing my job well," was correlated with both overall hospital rating and the HCAHPS question regarding receiving help toileting as soon as the patient wanted. The employee engagement question concerning the level of providing resources for employees to do their jobs effectively was strongly correlated with patients receiving help toileting as soon as wanted. The employee engagement question of stress level manageability was most correlated of all the questions with nurses treating patients with courtesy and respect. Lastly, employer recommendation was positively correlated with overall hospital rating from patients, as well as receiving call button help as soon as the patient wanted.

Overall, the most significant correlations reside in employee stress and employer recommendation. While other correlations have been positively noted, none are greater than that of stress and recommendation of employer. These factors have been significantly correlated to hospital rating, nursing courtesy and respect, and call button help. Arguably, call button assistance can be associated with empathy and compassion, key components to the patient-centered approach to care delivery.

In review of unit correlations, there is significant support of subculture and counterculture. Positive correlations with the overall organization in terms of patient experience resulted in only 31 percent among medical-surgical units, 28 percent of pediatric units, 20 percent of clinical sites, 17 percent of birthing units, and 12 percent of intensive care units.

The summation of the study points (based on analysis of standard deviation, p-value, and multiple regressions) to the most significant outcomes are outlined in the following text:

Results of Limited-to-No Correlation

1. There was no positive correlation between smaller hospitals associated with the collective system (hospitals with less than 6 percent of the total employee sample).

2. There was no positive correlation between the overall organization and the recently acquired health care system (five hospitals).

3. The measure of, "I would prefer to remain with this organization…" was negatively correlated with sustainable engagement while overall organizational satisfaction supported sustainable engagement.

Observations

1. Overall correlations within the commitment domain indicated preference to remain with an organization was not associated with commitment.

2. Having a sense of pride was marginally supportive of organizational commitment showing the two measures indicate limited correlation with commitment.

3. The statements, "I am able to sustain the level of energy I need through the day," "My work group operates effectively as a team," "I have a good understanding of how my job contributes to this organization achieving its mission, vision and strategic plan," and "The stress levels at work are usually manageable" indicate a weak correlation with sustainable engagement as an overall measure.

4. Analyses identified the organizational commitment domain to be improved by developing organizational pride and recommendation of the organization as an employer.

5. The sustainable engagement domain may be improved by improving organizational pride, satisfaction to remain employed with the organization, and recommendation as an employer.

6. Employer recommendation was positively correlated with overall hospital rating from patients, as well as receiving call button help as soon as the patient wanted.

Positive and Significant Correlations

1. The statements "There are no sustainable obstacles at work to doing my job well," "This organization provides the resources necessary for me to work effectively," and "I am proud to work for or to be affiliated with this organization," all have positive correlations with sustainable engagement measures.

2. Organizational pride and recommending the organization as a good place to work is significantly correlated with organizational commitment (separately measured domain).

Most Notable Correlations

1. The most significant correlations reside in employee stress and employer recommendation. While other correlations have been positively noted, none are greater than that of stress and recommendation of employer. These factors have been significantly correlated to hospital rating, nursing courtesy and respect, and call button help.

2. Recommendation of the employer was correlated with measures of overall hospital rating, patients receiving call button help as soon as wanted, and nurses listening carefully to patients. Overall satisfaction with the employer was strongly correlated with overall hospital rating, as was the overall commitment domain.

3. The employee engagement statement, "There are no substantial obstacles at work to doing my job well," was correlated with both overall hospital rating and the HCAHPS question regarding receiving help toileting as soon as the patient wanted.

4. The employee engagement question concerning the level of providing resources for employees to do their jobs effectively was strongly correlated with patients receiving help toileting as soon as wanted.

5. The employee engagement question of stress level manageability was most correlated of all questions with nurses treating patients with courtesy and respect.

Analysis and Interpretation

With so much analysis of correlations and observations, it is easy to become overwhelmed with so much information. However, the results of the health care culture and patient feedback study arms leaders and practitioners with a significant amount of knowledge; each observation must be broken down into digestible summaries. Through the results presented, there are several conclusions that may be drawn to describe the behavioral contribution of employees. As a reminder, the questionnaire is located in Appendix C.

Results of Limited-to-No Correlation

The observational study presented three areas of limited-to-no correlation. First, there was no positive correlation between smaller hospitals in employee engagement with the overall health system. This result was derived from measuring smaller systems that individually was composed of less than 6 percent of the overall employee sample. Second, there was no positive correlation between the overall organization and the recently acquired health system. Interestingly, during the time of data collection and observation, a second, unaffiliated organization was purchased by the parent system. Third, the measure of employee preference to remain with their employer was negatively correlated with sustainable engagement though overall organizational satisfaction supported by sustainable engagement.

The findings within this section indicate that a lack of cultural connection exists in critical access hospitals. This is a level of cultural independence that exists in a subculture (as outlined in previous chapters), distinguishing employee experience and feedback from the rest of the organization. Second, the findings identify no correlation between the overall health system and the recently acquired health care system (composed of five campuses). This finding supports the assumed outcome that external cultures exist, though in the same socioeconomic dynamics, apart from other similar organizations. When large organizations acquire other large organizations, it is expected that culture will exist in a separate manner (for many years), as identified in the results of this study. Third, the measurement in assessing stay intention among health system employees was found to be negatively correlated with sustainable engagement though overall satisfaction supported sustainable engagement. A result of this type provides two key areas of insight. First, stay intention is a measure incapable, within the workgroup surveyed, of contributing to identifying engagement. Second, stay intention and overall organizational satisfaction are not related in a manner that may be operationally acted upon or measurably assessed. If stay intention is not an outcome of engagement, additional measures should be put in place to understand why stay intention was negatively correlated with engagement. There is, like identified earlier in the service organization, an underlying motivation factor associated with satisfaction and engagement. Bear in mind the knowledge that motivation factors among workgroups are exceedingly capable of influencing multiple domains of employee engagement.

Observations

Within the observations section, overall correlations associated with the commitment domain indicated there is no relationship between the desire to remain with an organization and the overall commitment domain measures. Having a sense of pride was marginally supportive of organization commitment, showing the measures of stay intention and pride are not correlated in the instrument domain of commitment. Energy level, team effectiveness, and understanding how an employee's role contributes to organizational success, as well as how manageable stress levels are shows minimal correlation with sustainable engagement. The resulting question surfacing from observation seeks to understand, "*How are these measures valid?*" Results provide insight that organizational commitment, within the subject organization, may be improved by developing organizational pride and employee recommendations of the organization as an employer. The sustainable engagement domain may be improved through enhancing organizational pride, satisfaction to remain employed, and recommendation of the employer.

Positive and Significant Correlations

Positive and significant correlations provide insight to organizational culture and behavior. The question of sustainable obstacles for an employee to do his or her job well, resource availability to adequately perform, and organizational pride were all positively correlated to the Sustainable Engagement domain. Organizational Pride and Recommendation of the Organization as a good place to work was significantly correlated with organizational commitment, though commitment and sustainable engagement were separately measured. Through this view, the health care system is capable of improving organizational commitment and stay intention by improving performance obstacles and resources. Interestingly, organizational pride, resources, and obstacles are not included in organizational commitment, though the correlation remains positive. This exhibits a significant opportunity to improve stay intention for the health system.

Most Notable Correlations

It is within the most notable correlations that insight develops and provides influence and impact on end users (patients) in health care. There are five key areas of analysis within the study on health care bedside employee engagement and patient experience feedback. First, the most significant correlations reside in employee stress and employer recommendation. Clearly, through the results presented, employees with higher levels of workplace stress have higher levels of unfavorable recommendations from their employer. To compound the issue from the patient perspective, high levels of stress directly influence hospital rating, nursing courtesy, nursing respect, and call button help. Though these measures are pragmatic in their outcomes, the significant outcome from the patient perspective is the question regarding receiving help as soon as needed when pressing a call button. Empathy naturally erodes when employees are stressed and detached from patient needs leading to patient button response delays with limited empathy for patients.

As outlined previously, employer recommendation holds many correlations. In fact, recommendation of the health system employer was significantly correlated with measures of overall patient hospital ratings as well as the call button response and nurses listening carefully to patients. Returning to obstacles, the employee engagement question associated with obstacles from doing one's job well was significantly correlated with patient responses of receiving toileting as soon as wanted. In the organizational measure of resource accessibility, toileting was again correlated in an unfavorable measure for patients. Lastly, and most correlated of all, stress among health care professionals was found to directly influence treating patients with courtesy and respect.

CHAPTER 9

Model and Application

Knowledge, learning, and education are all wonderful things when they are used and applied to careers, daily life, health, and relationships. This book, till this point, has provided significant information regarding workplace motivation factors, organizational commitment, cultural perspectives, case studies, and analyses. The next task is to apply the vast constructs to specific teams and groups. In order to do so, the author will discuss a theoretical model that the author has developed to apply to any work group, team, and organization to identify workplace dynamics with interpretations and measures. With that said, he added the caveat of "it depends."

When the author was in graduate school, he had a law professor that continuously pushed the phrase of "it depends." When considering law and legislation, it is all situationally relevant. *When is someone guilty? When is an action justified? Who determines it is right or wrong?* Truly, "*it depends.*" The author says this because instruments, tools, models, theories, and measures can provide objective measures, but not subjective assumptions and interpretations. As you walk through the model the author proposes, he asks you to keep in mind that all workplaces, teams, and individuals exist to varying degrees within cultures where they create, participate, and withdraw. The model the author proposes will provide insight and guidance, but like all theoretical models, it will not autonomously describe all of the characteristics and dynamics of your team.

Revisiting Constructs

Workplace Motivation

Workplace motivation, as presented in Chapter 2, is composed of intrinsic and extrinsic motivation factors. Intrinsic motivation includes the following factors:

- Role challenge
- Recognition for work completed
- Control over ones role, schedule, and workflow
- Cooperation with peers and leaders
- Employee aspirations, curiosity, and fantasy
- Goal and performance achievement
- The work itself
- Responsibility
- Advancement and growth
- Goal-setting
- Workplace learning
- Role variety

Extrinsic motivation factors include:

- Company policies
- Performance hindrance
- Supervisor relationships
- Supervisor quality
- Relationships with peers
- Peer performance quality
- Workplace conditions
- Workplace safety
- Salary and wages
- Position status
- Job security
- Workplace competition

Intrinsic factors are those that motivate the presence of a factor and have a motivational influence among employees contributing to satisfaction. Extrinsic factors are those that contribute to dissatisfaction when absent while the presence of extrinsic factors does not equate to increased job satisfaction. Essentially, when these factors are absent, there is a contribution to dissatisfaction among employees, though the presence of each factor does not lead to job satisfaction.

As outlined in Chapter 2, motivation is the force in the workplace driving all employee behavior where employees are motivated in different ways. My Tri-Factor Model of Motivation, Commitment and Culture has been developed with Herzberg's theory of workplace motivation in mind. Intrinsic and extrinsic factors have been developed in an assessment to provide leaders with insight into the type of motivation and subfactor type to identify motivational themes (relationships, wages, advancement, etc.). When evaluating the complexity of workplace motivation, individual needs vary through attitudes, perceptions, education levels, and personality. Intrinsic motivation may lead to increased individual output with a positive effect on morale, productivity, satisfaction, and efficiency. Dissatisfaction among employees may result from the absence of extrinsic factors in areas of company policy, supervision, relationships, salary, and job status. As outlined in the opening of this book, if motivation factors are not understood and addressed, turnover and adverse outcomes perpetually ensue. Organizational leaders must be able to, at a minimum, understand and counter balance workplace motivation with development of motivation factors. If employees are extrinsically motivated, the environment must develop extrinsic factors in the same way intrinsic factors must be satisfied.

Organizational Commitment

Organizational commitment is more than half a century old as a theoretical construct. Essentially, contemporary observations and conclusions have found three types of commitment: *affective, continuance,* and *normative.* For the sake of the proposed model and identifying types, the author remains oriented on *affective* and *continuance* commitment. Affective organizational commitment is based on the emotional attachment, participation, and involvement an employee has with an organization. Continuance organizational commitment is based on necessity, dependency, and personal sacrifice because of various reasons that motivate an employee to remain with his or her employer. Limitations and dependency of continuance commitment may be the result of geographic, educational, skill, and familial restrictions and demands. The four models proposed in contemporary research identify relationships between commitment and satisfaction as job satisfaction which leads to commitment, commitment leads to satisfaction, satisfaction and commitment affect each other, and commitment and satisfaction are independent. Moreover, in the study presented earlier on service workers in health care, affective commitment was directly correlated with intrinsic motivation while continuance commitment was correlated with extrinsic motivation factor presence.

In the proposed Tri-Factor Model, measures and analyses are presented through emotionally-based and individually motivated factors influencing the connection between each form of commitment. When placed in conjunction with motivation in the same model, leaders are able to identify ways to improve stay intention and commitment among employees by way of validated outcomes in relationships between motivation and commitment.

Culture and Subculture

Subculture, culture, and attribution, as presented in Chapter 4, are highly indicative and useful for both motivation and commitment. Understanding subculture (cultural sub- and cultural independency) and organizational culture among groups (cultural dependency) supports identifying pockets of motivation and commitment; independent culture groups hold varying degrees of each. When a leader is able to identify the strength of a subculture, as opposed to consistency with organizational culture, motivation factors and commitment become more fragile as they are directly associated with the culture of the workgroup. With the factors of culture and subculture outlined in Chapter 4, the next objective surrounds measuring and evaluating culture. In order to measure culture, two dimensions may be employed: employee surveys based on motivation and commitment, as well as on visual observations.

When measuring cultural characteristics, leaders should consider visible guiding principles to determine behavior and structures in the social interactions within the organization, including customer orientation, service excellence, and teamwork (Schmiedel et al. 2013). Within the substrata of cultural measures and evaluation, internal perspectives (motivation and commitment measures), improvement and innovation (individual, team, and organizational key performance indicators), accountability (organizational commitment and internal performance assessments), commitment, and structures (employee engagement survey targeted themes) can be evaluated for depth and presence. Organizational culture has become a significant element in organizational research where behaviors, when accurately assessed and measured, can be linked to outcomes associated with job satisfaction, engagement, and goal achievement. With the multidimensional approach of measuring cultural variables by way of motivation factors, employee engagement, and organizational commitment, results provide links in the organizational culture and performance.

Additional factors for identification of cultural depth and presence include measurement of beliefs and ethical behaviors supporting norms in the workplace environment. Dimensional factors and themes are essential in targeting specific groups of responses. While employee survey assessments seem to understand various factors, including organizational pride, teamwork, leadership, development opportunities, and organizational trust, surveys are most valuable when the approach is based on themes, such as sustainable engagement (affective commitment), employer of choice (motivation and commitment), environment of teamwork (motivation), growth opportunities (motivation), and employment benefits (extrinsic motivation). The ultimate objective should be to incorporate themes and dimensions that capture intrinsic and extrinsic motivation while also being able to place a measure on affective and continuance organizational commitment.

Tri-Factor Model: Motivation, Commitment, and Culture

To lay the groundwork of common definitions, the Tri-Factor Model of Motivation, Commitment and Culture is based upon, the following factors:

1. *Intrinsic motivation factors:* Factors related to value congruence and connectedness with an organization; conduct and behavior depend on feeling motivated for personal reasons and rewards (Fareed and Jan 2016).

2. *Extrinsic motivation factors:* Factors related to pay, working conditions, and supervisors; behavior is driven by employees' desire to gain recognition or reward or to avoid punishment or negative judgment (Fareed and Jan 2016).

3. *Affective organizational commitment:* The emotional attachment, identification, and involvement that an individual has with his or her organization (McShane et al. 2009).

4. *Continuance organizational commitment:* Commitment to an organization based on personal sacrifice and the necessity to remain employed because of limitations in available options (Lapointe and Vandenberghe 2018).

5. *Cultural depth and presence*: Cultural richness refers to the level of presence of culturally related employee behaviors as measured through bedside care employees.

6. *Organizational culture*: Organizational culture is the special collection of shared norms and values by individuals and groups in the organization that control the way interactions occur (Moss et al. 2017).

7. *Operational culture*: The aspects of the organizational culture that influence outcomes associated with employee performance, driven by behavioral components of organizational culture. Organizational and individual actions inversely influence the culture of the organization.

8. *Subculture*: A culturally connected group operating within a larger culture with shared beliefs, interests, attitudes, and values on a more isolated level that may or may not be consistent with the larger culture. The subculture group is typically derived from the overall organizational culture in workplace settings.

Model Factors

The Tri-Factor Model of Motivation, Commitment and Culture also incorporates the motivation factors and commitment characteristics listed in Tables 9.1 and 9.2. In terms of culture and subculture measures (as shown in Table 9.3), results may be used on a scale or presence-based perspective to determine the degree to which a culture positively or

Table 9.1 *Motivation factors*

Intrinsic factors	Extrinsic factors
Role challenge	Company policies
Recognition for work completed	Performance hindrances
Control over role	Supervisor relationships
Cooperation with peers and leaders	Supervisor quality
Employee aspirations, curiosity, and fantasy	Relationships with peers
Goal and performance achievement	Peer performance
The work itself	Workplace conditions
Responsibility	Workplace safety
Advancement and growth	Position status
Goal-setting	Salary and wages
Role variety	Workplace competition

Table 9.2 *Organizational commitment factors*

Affective commitment	Continuance commitment
Personal meaning and purpose	Limited alternative employment options
Belonging/family feeling	Personal investment
Emotional attachment	Lacking options to leave employer
Conviction to stay with employer	Life disruption if leaves employer
Problem sharing	Unable to leave employer when employee wants to
Stay intention	Stay necessity

Table 9.3 *Organizational operating culture and subculture factors*

Organizational culture	Subculture
Subculture influence	Group intra-cultural ties
Workplace shared values	Group sharing of values
Workplace shared beliefs	Group share of tasks
Workplace role consistency	Group share of burdens
Workplace skill consistency	Group share of education/skill
Workplace role rules	Group autonomy

negatively exists, as well as how "pocketed" culture may be in support-ing subcultures. For this reason, the author strongly emphasizes the ap-proach of employee surveys with themes and dimensions as outlined previously.

Tri-Factor Model of Motivation, Commitment, and Culture

The Tri-Factor Model of Motivation, Commitment, and Culture is displayed in Figure 9.1. The model uses a scale approach to determine the dimensions in which employees, workgroups, departments, and organizations may be measured to provide a visual indication of most important factors. Each dimension is utilized and applied using the three descriptions provided earlier in this chapter. Both center access points for each access are essentially balancing points for applying factors while end points are the "all or nothing" baselines. Diagram interpretations are outlined in Figure 9.1. Additionally, the model is applied to workplace turnover to identify shortcomings, opportunities, and retention development. Lastly, it is important to note that there is no greater value in each scale; −4.0 and +4.0 have no prescriptive outcomes and are points on a scale.

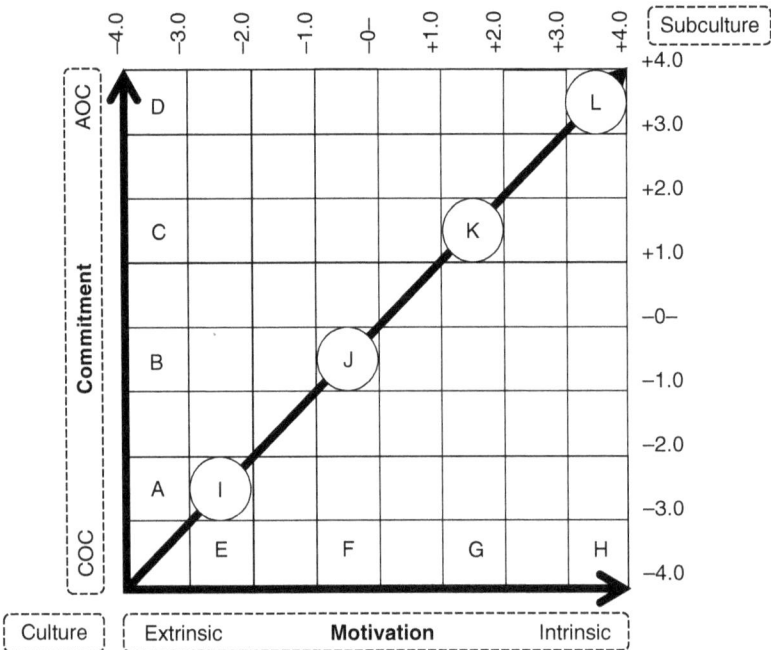

Figure 9.1 Tri-Factor Model

Model Interpretations

Motivation Factors

Extrinsic motivation factors in the Tri-Factor Model begin on the bottom left at −4.0. The "E" range of motivation factors is a measure indicating significant extrinsic motivation among the worker(s), teams, or organizations evaluated. Recalling the listing of extrinsic motivation factors in Table 9.1, factors include salary and wages, position status, workplace relationships, and organizational policies. When you scale the motivation section, bear in mind that some factors are more influential than others. For example, if there is workforce turnover and the focus is on pay, benefits, and perks, the extrinsic factor of salary and wages would place a stronghold on the −4.0 range while position status, relationships, and workplace conditions will have a lesser impact on extrinsic motivation. Thus, it may be helpful to scale the items in extrinsic motivation as they relate to your workforce. An example is provided in the following text. Depending on employee observations, surveys, and assessments, each factor can be weighted to identify stronger factors of motivation.

- Salary and wages (−4.0)
- Peer performance (−3.5)
- Supervisor relationships (−3.0)
- Workplace aspects (−2.5, each)
- Position status (−2.0)
- And so forth

The same process may be applied to intrinsic motivation through the factors provided in Table 9.1. In the intrinsic scale, measures are inverse to those of the extrinsic type. The strongest intrinsic motivation is measured at a +4.0. Intrinsic and extrinsic factors in the model exist on a continuum with a single point of balance, rather than with two points per axis. Again, placing a weighted value on each factor can support identifying motivation through assessments, observations, and surveying of employees. See the simplified example that follows:

- Role challenge (+4.0)
- Advancement and growth opportunities (+3.75)
- The work itself/role fulfillment (+3.5)
- Role variety (+2.5)
- Responsibility (+2.5)
- Recognition (+1.5)
- And so forth

Once the factors are weighted, based on observations, assessments, and surveying, a more accurate measure may be placed on each dimension. After weighting each factor, the model employs an average of factors. For example, consider the following:

- Salary and wages is measured as significant in extrinsic factors (-4.0)
- Position status is significantly rated in extrinsic factors (-2.0)
- Role challenge is rated highly in intrinsic motivation ($+4.0$)
- Role variety is highly rated in intrinsic motivation ($+2.5$)
- Recognition is highly rated in intrinsic motivation ($+1.5$)

The resulting measure, as identified in Figure 9.2 equates to 2.0 on the intrinsic scale.

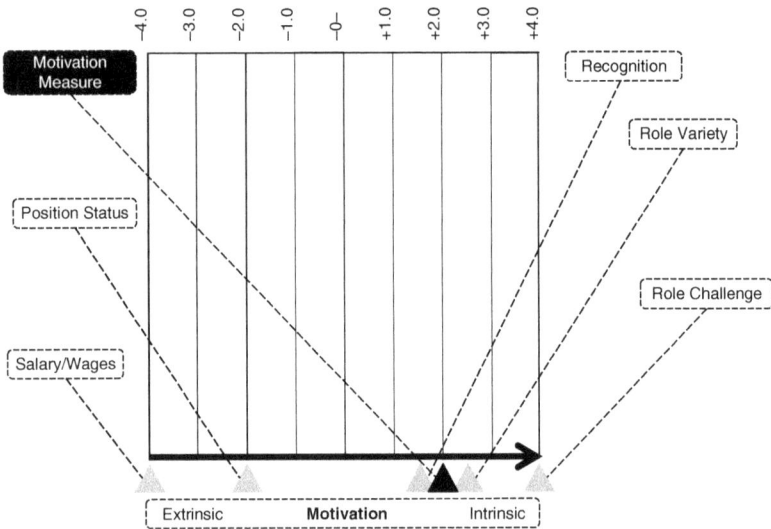

Figure 9.2 Motivation factors measure example

With the first of three dimensions done, we will now shift the focus to organizational commitment.

Organizational Commitment

Organizational commitment is based on continuance commitment and affective commitment, as outlined in Table 9.2 and Chapter 3. Continuance organizational commitment is based on the *y-axis* at -4.0; affective organizational commitment exists at +4.0 on the commitment scale. In the commitment scale, the author proposes a specific measure of averages based on each dimension among the workforce as commitment is based on different dimensions, rather than on a scale with weights of +4.0 to +1.0 for affective commitment and −4.0 to −1.0 for continuance commitment. At this point, it is important to introduce normative organizational commitment in a more thorough manner. As outlined in Chapter 3, normative organizational commitment depends on employee loyalty, stay obligation, and commitment to membership providing reciprocal valued benefits by belonging to, or being a part of, an organization (Lapointe and Vandenberghe 2018). It is through this third dimension of organizational commitment that midpoints of the scale (−1.0 to +1.0) may be incorporated to offset commitment characteristics among the workforce where each measure is divided by 3. Normative organizational commitment is outlined below in Table 9.4.

Table 9.4 Normative organizational commitment factors

Stay intention driven by individual desire
Stay intention driven by justified resignation (feeling it is disrespectful to resign, for example)
Guilt for resignation
Organization deserves employee loyalty
Obligation to remain in organization for peers and others in the organization
Personal investment that is emotionally and physically due to an employer

As an example for determining the scale measure for organizational commitment, see Figure 9.3. In the example, the workforce demonstrated all six factors of affective commitment, eight factors of normative commitment, and two factors of continuance commitment. Given that there are six factors per dimension, the net sum calculation should never result in less, or more, than +/− six items. In the example, the workforce under review exhibited stay intentions in affective commitment of 4; there were 2 identifiers in continuance factors and 4 normative commitment identifiers.

Culture and Subculture

Culture and subculture are composed of a multitude of items for measurement, observation, and assessment. To keep variables relevant, as well as outlining these two factor constructs in a dichotomy, the author has

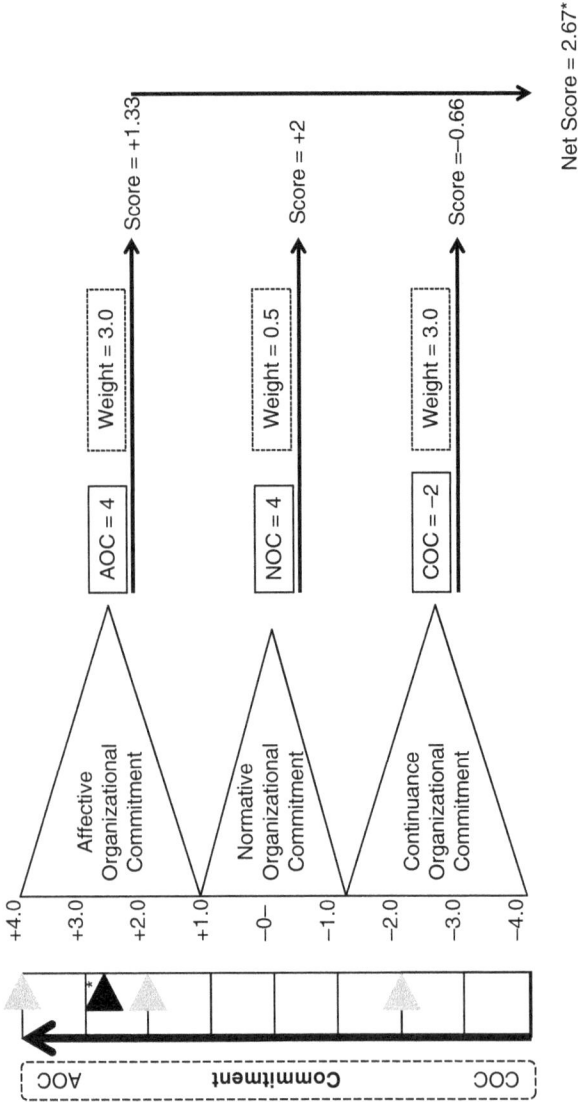

Figure 9.3 Organizational commitment measures

outlined factors as presented in Table 9.4. Organizational and operational culture is, on the most basic levels, persuaded by the influence a sub-culture holds on organizational culture, basic shared values and beliefs, role consistency across the organization, skill consistency across the organization, and the barriers of workplace rules affecting a specific role(s). Subculture is central to group dynamics, including cultural ties within an operating organizational culture, sharing of values, role similarity, task and burden consistency, skill and educational requirement consistency, and the ability (or choice) for the group to operate at an autonomous level in a way that may be inconsistent with the overall organizational culture.

As before, a weighted approach is necessary for the relevant work-force to measure influence and measures to understand the identifying factors associated with the culture dimension of the Tri-Factor Model. In Figure 9.4, weights have been applied as outlined in the following list. The overall average result indicates favorability to an overall cultural value of +2.0. To reemphasize, the surveying method and weights must be applied based on the relevant workforce; organizations are unique in commitment, motivation, and cultural dynamics.

- Shared Values and Beliefs: -0-
- Organizational Cultural Dependency: −1.0
- Group Culture Exceeding Organizational Culture: +4.0
- Group Sharing for Values, Tasks and Burdens: +3.0
- Small Group Ability to Work Autonomously: +2.0

Multifactor Model Measures

With the Tri-Factor Model examples provided, each measure may be applied to understand the outcomes of a workgroup while weighing the desired outcomes against actual measures. Each factor is applied below through the factors outlined in Tables 9.2, 9.3, and 9.4. From this, the model provided in Figure 9.1 is applied as a descriptive model.

Figure 9.2 identified Motivation as a +2.0, Figure 9.3 identified Commitment as a +2.67, while Figure 9.4 identified Culture as a +2.0 measure. In this measure, as shown in Figure 9.5, derived from Figure 9.1, results show a D, K, and G. Referencing Figure 9.1, a D

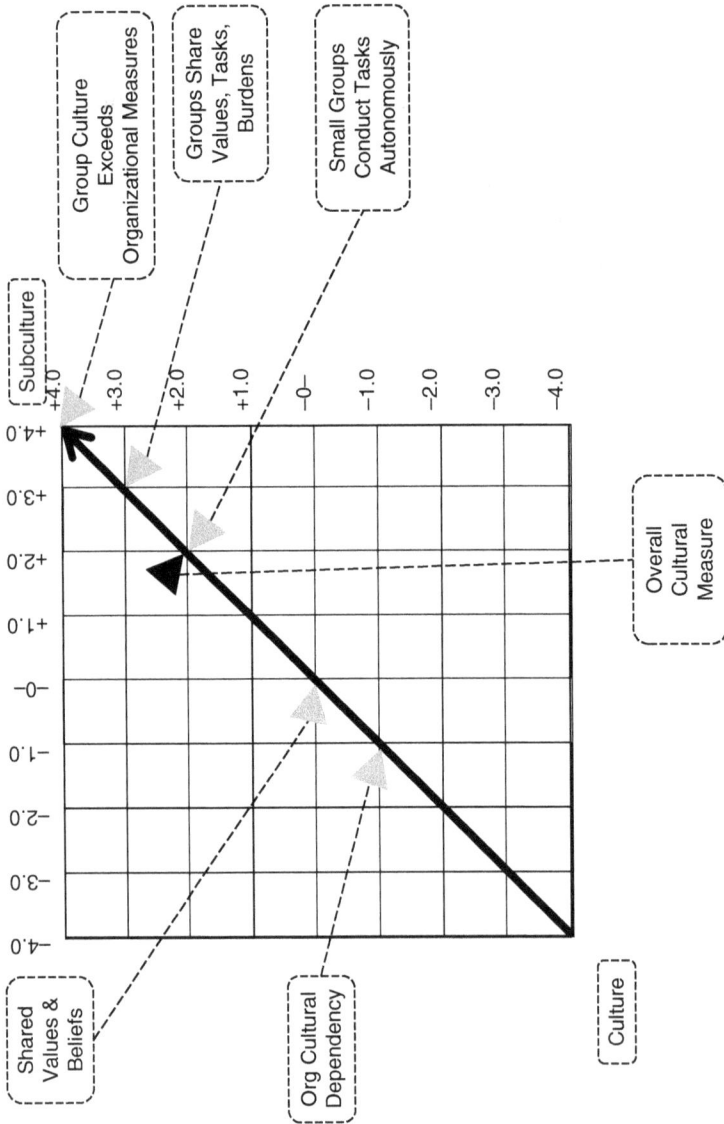

Figure 9.4 *Organizational culture measures*

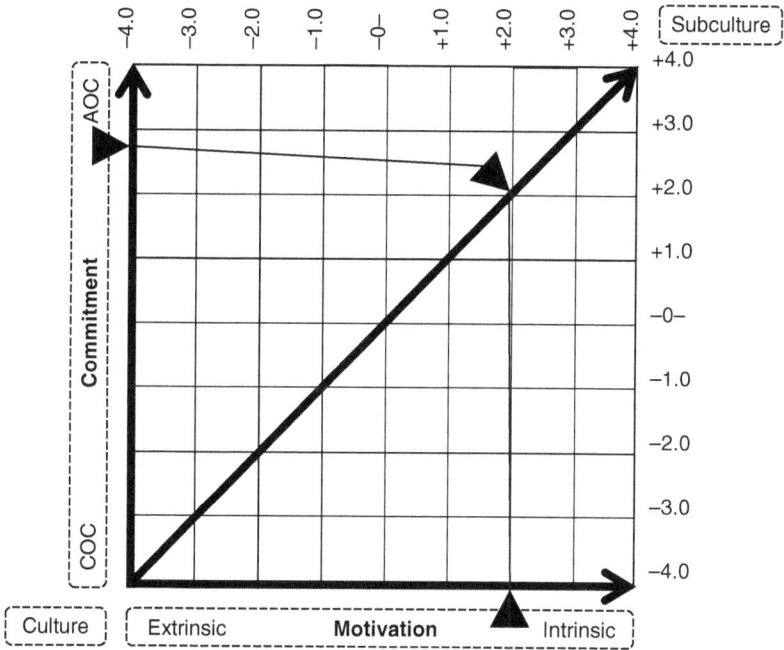

Figure 9.5 Organizational commitment measures

measure (+2.67 out of −4.0 to +4.0) indicates a high level of affective organizational commitment. In workgroups with exceptionally high levels of this type of commitment, motivations to support the continuity of commitment, while continuing to enhance commitment, include cultural measures and intrinsic motivation factors. Higher levels of intrinsic motivation, as presented in the health care service worker study, positively correlate with higher affective commitment, thus, providing role challenges, recognition, worker autonomy, professional development, growth opportunities, and environments supporting cooperation and collaboration among employees to achieve common goals and tasks. When intrinsic motivation factors are present, affective organizational commitment is supported through factor support of developing personal meaning and purpose, belonging, stay intention, problem solving, and meaningful work.

Consistently, a G measure of motivation factors (+2.0; reference Figure 9.1) supports significant intrinsic factor motivation. The correlation between affective commitment and intrinsic motivation go hand in hand with the motivation and factor relationship described in the earlier paragraphs. Additionally, workforces with high levels of intrinsic motivation require the consistent presence of challenges, recognition, autonomy, collaboration, growth, development, variety, and responsibility. The workgroups are not necessarily motivated by policy, relationships, position status, wages, and peer performance. However, extrinsic factor absence, as outlined in Herzberg's model, does not equate to dissatisfaction. The key to the workforce in Figure 9.5 is to continue to drive the intrinsic factors in Table 9.1 and commitment factors in Table 9.2.

Lastly, the cultural measure of the example workforce supports a measure of K (+2.0; see Figure 9.1). Significant results supporting subculture identify two different areas of analysis. First, the organization has an implied dependency on subcultures. This requires an assessment of the subculture dynamics to understand in what areas the organization can rely on subculture groups to drive organizational values. With the affective commitment and intrinsic motivation of the example workforce, an early observation would suggest learning and development, career advancement, strategy, problem solving, and workforce collaboration as the factors of subculture motivation. Second, the identification of a strong level of subculture suggests the example workforce operates in pockets of workgroups with similarity in task burden, education, values, and group autonomy. In order to exert an organizational level of cultural development, organizational leadership will face needs to normalize the culture on a full organizational level that embraces areas of diversity and employee engagement. A comprehensive assessment of the culture and employee surveying would provide insight to opportunities to balance the culture. That being said, an imbalanced culture is not necessarily a negative thing. An organization that is exploding in growth with a strong professional development subculture will absolutely depend on the subculture to spread to the greater workforce. Conversely, if the organization is growing and the strong presence of subculture is full of individuals motivated by stay intention over growth and development, the organization will be significantly challenged to enhance and build an experienced workforce. Rather, the organization might have to seek external resources and recruitment to meet the demands of growth.

The Tri-Factor Model Applied to Turnover

The Tri-Factor Model can be applied to workforce turnover to identify factor considerations leading to turnover. In order to demonstrate this, the author will provide analysis from a case study organization.

Service Organization from Chapter Two

A review of the case study:

> In a 2018 private sector services employer case study the author conducted, turnover rates exceeded 50 percent. Turnover was as high as an average of 13.7 employees per day, annualized. When reviewing the causes for leaving among former employees completing an exit interview survey, participants rated the company 72.3 percent favorable as an employer. 57 percent of participants were employed less than 2 years, 40 percent were employed 2–5 years, and 3 percent were employed greater than 5 years. 82 percent of respondents report teamwork was strong, 42 percent left the employer due to higher paying employment alternatives, 38 percent left for "something else," 12 percent left because of poor management and 8% percent left because of physical demands.

In review of these factors:

- 72.3 percent rated the employer as favorable (intrinsically driven)
- 82 percent reported teamwork was strong (extrinsic factor)
- 42 percent left the employer for higher pay (extrinsic factor)
- 38 percent left for 'something else'
- 12 percent left because of poor management (extrinsic factor)
- 8 percent left because of physical demands (extrinsic factor)

The concerned organization advertised that employment and training would be full of opportunities for growth (intrinsic), professional development (intrinsic), and role variety (intrinsic). While the organization performed very well in reinforcing intrinsic factors, it employed individuals that were extrinsically motivated. While there is no fault in seeking strategy in enhancing intrinsic motivation, if the organization does not address extrinsically motivated workforces, turnover will perpetually occur. This is outlined in Figure 9.6.

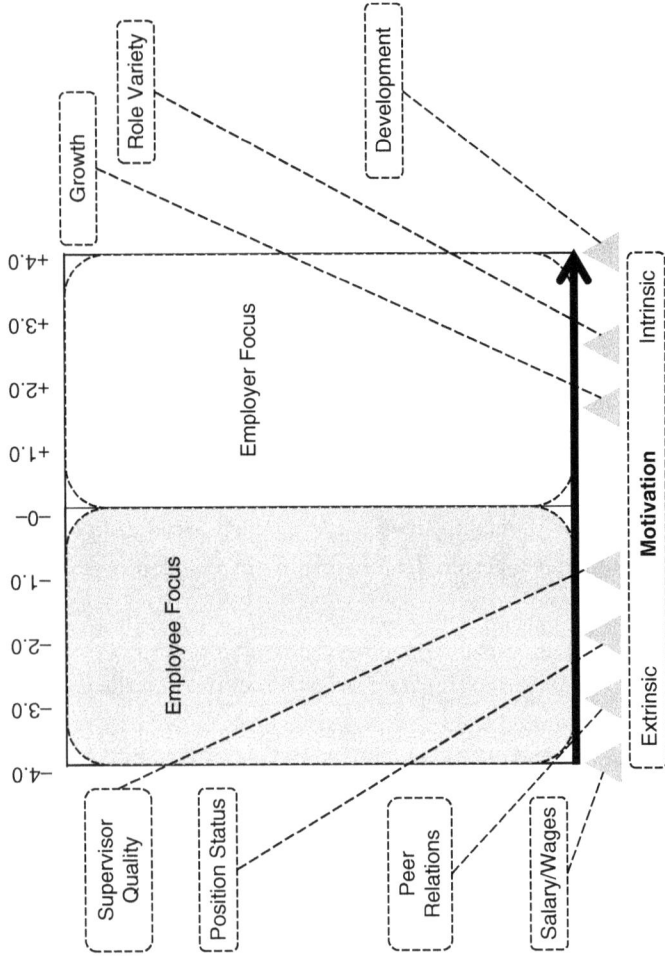

Figure 9.6 Tri-Factor Model applied to turnover and employer–employee focus

Figure 9.6 uses motivation factors to identify the focus between the employer and the employee perspectives. The case study is an analysis providing a clear approach to the differences between the two sides of employment. Similar approaches may be applied to commitment and culture. The key is to differentiate what factors are important to employees and what factors are required from employers.

CHAPTER 10

Leading and Managing within Constructs

Leadership is composed of a multitude of behavioral dynamics. Leaders have values as diverse as those of the workforces they employ. For alignment of employees and leaders, the author recommends another of his books, *The Optimized Leader*. However, the bottom line is determining the workforce you should seek to employ and manage alongside the actual employees you have. The management approach must be shifted to developing a workplace consistent with your fit in motivation factors, commitment, and culture. This book, to this point, has provided several background studies on employee motivation and commitment. However, there are some key points of consideration for the practitioner. *What kind of workforce do you employ? What is your industry? What is important to your employees? What is important to you? Do these constructs align?*

Motivation

Motivation factors must align between workplace values and employee values to ensure performance, retention, and success (see Table 10.1). It is critically important to ensure these factors consistently exhibit and communicate the same message. As outlined before, when motivation is not sufficiently met between the employee and the factors an employer supports, turnover and adverse outcomes will perpetuate.

Commitment

Commitment, as outlined, is positively correlated between intrinsic motivation and affective commitment. It is crucial to ensure that the factors

Table 10.1 Motivation factors

Intrinsic factors	Extrinsic factors
Role challenge	Company policies
Recognition for work completed	Performance hindrances
Control over role	Supervisor relationships
Cooperation with peers and leaders	Supervisor quality
Employee aspirations, curiosity, and fantasy	Relationships with peers
Goal and performance achievement	Peer performance
The work itself	Workplace conditions
Responsibility	Workplace safety
Advancement and growth	Position status
Goal-setting	Salary and wages
Role variety	Workplace competition

that motivate organizational commitment are aligned with motivation factors. When a mismatch occurs, turnover and adverse shortcomings will remain a perpetual challenge (see Table 10.2).

Table 10.2 Organizational commitment factors

Affective commitment	Continuance commitment
Personal meaning and purpose	Limited alternative employment options
Belonging/family feeling	Personal investment
Emotional attachment	Lacking options to leave employer
Conviction to stay with employer	Life disruption if leaves employer
Problem sharing	Unable to leave employer when employee wants to
Stay intention	Stay necessity

Culture

Lastly, culture holds many variable dynamics of independence and dependency. Organizational objectives, strategy, and goals must be weighed against the level of cultural measures within a workforce. Chapter 9 outlined the various considerations, based on measures. However, it is the leadership approach to identify and apply motivation factors and commitment to balance organizational dependency on cultural measures. Table 10.3 identifies factors related to cultural measures.

Table 10.3 Organizational operating culture and subculture factors

Organizational culture	Subculture
Subculture influence	Group intra-cultural ties
Workplace shared values	Group sharing of values
Workplace shared beliefs	Group sharing of tasks
Workplace role consistency	Group sharing of burdens
Workplace skill consistency	Group sharing of education/skill
Workplace role rules	Group autonomy

Moving Forward

At this point, after review of multiple case studies and research studies, it is now up to you, as a leader, to determine what you want to measure, how you want to obtain measures, and what you do with those measures. What do you want these items to be? Do those items fit with your leadership? Do they fit with your employer? Do they fit with your mission? And, most of all, do they fit with your workforce?

Management and leadership is a journey. How you align the factors of managing and leading the human element is the journey ahead.

APPENDIX A

Motivation Factors and Affective Commitment Survey Instrument

---

2. Workplace Motivators

Please select the most appropriate response as it relates to your current place of employment.

* 2. I feel there is a good chance I'll be promoted

  ◯ This factor is not present

  ◯ This factor is present, but is not important

  ◯ This factor is fairly important

  ◯ This factor is of major importance

* 3. I receive a particularly challenging assignment.

  ◯ This factor was not present

  ◯ This factor was present but not important

  ◯ This factor is fairly important

  ◯ This factor was of major importance

* 4. A job I did received recognition in was a particularly good piece of work.

  ◯ This factor was not present

  ◯ The factor was present but was not important

  ◯ This factor was fairly important

  ◯ This factor was of major importance

* 5. The working relationship I have with my supervisor is very good.

  ◯ This factor was not present

  ◯ This factor was present but was not important

  ◯ This factor was fairly important

  ◯ This factor was of major importance

* 6. The working relationship I have with co-workers at my level is very good.

  ◯ This factor was not present

  ◯ This factor was present but not important

  ◯ This factor was fairly important

  ◯ This factor was of significant importance

* 7. I am working under a supervisor who really knows his job.

○ This factor was not present

○ This factor was present but now was important

○ This factor was fairly important

○ This factor was of major importance

* 8. I am expecting (or received) a merit increase.

○ This factor was not present

○ This factor was present but was not important

○ This factor was fairly important

○ This factor was of major importance

* 9. I have a real feeling of achievement in the work I am doing.

○ This factor was not present

○ The factor was present but was not important

○ The factor was fairly important

○ The factor was of major importance

* 10. I have exceptionally good working conditions and equipment.

○ This factor was not present

○ This factor was present but was not important

○ This factor was fairly important

○ This factor was of major importance

* 11. I am given increased responsibility in my job.

○ This factor was not present

○ This factor was present but no important

○ This factor was fairly important

○ This factor was of major importance

* 12. I feel secure in my job.

- ( ) This factor was not present

- ( ) This factor was present but was not important

- ( ) This factor was fairly important

- ( ) This factor was of major importance

* 13. I am getting training and experience on the job that is helping my growth.

- ( ) This factor was not present

- ( ) This factor was present but was not important

- ( ) This factor is fairly important

- ( ) This factor is of major importance

* 14. The company improved an employee benefit program that is of importance to me.

- ( ) This factor in not present

- ( ) This factor is present but is not important

- ( ) This factor is fairly important

- ( ) This factor is of major importance

* 15. I like the kind of work I am doing.

- ( ) This factor is not present

- ( ) This factor is present but is not important

- ( ) This factor is fairly important

- ( ) This factor is of major importance

* 16. My job situation has changed in such a way that it has improved my home life.

- ( ) This factor is not present

- ( ) This factor is present but is not important

- ( ) This factor is fairly important

- ( ) This factor is of major importance

* 17. I am working in a group that operates smoothly and efficiently.

  ○ This factor is not present

  ○ This factor is present but is not important

  ○ This factor is fairly important

  ○ This factor is of major importance

* 18. Management policies affecting my work group takes into consideration the personal feelings of employees.

  ○ This factor is not present

  ○ This factor is present but is not important

  ○ This factor is fairly important

  ○ This factor is of major importance

* 19. This job required the use of my best abilities.

  ○ This factor is not present

  ○ This factor is present but is not important

  ○ This factor is fairly important

  ○ This factor is of major importance

4. Demographics - About You

* 38. What is your gender?

○ Female

○ Male

* 39. What is your age?

○ 17 or younger

○ 18-20

○ 21-29

○ 30-39

○ 40-49

○ 50-59

○ 60 or older

* 40. About how long have you been in your current position?

Years	
Months	

APPENDIX B

HCAHPS Survey Instrument

HCAHPS Survey

SURVEY INSTRUCTIONS

♦ You should only fill out this survey if you were the patient during the hospital stay named in the cover letter. Do not fill out this survey if you were not the patient.

♦ Answer <u>all</u> the questions by checking the box to the left of your answer.

♦ You are sometimes told to skip over some questions in this survey. When this happens you will see an arrow with a note that tells you what question to answer next, like this:

    ☐   Yes
    ☑   No   ➔ *If No, Go to Question 1*

> *You may notice a number on the survey. This number is used to let us know if you returned your survey so we don't have to send you reminders.*
> *Please note: Questions 1-25 in this survey are part of a national initiative to measure the quality of care in hospitals. OMB #0938-0981*

Please answer the questions in this survey about your stay at the hospital named on the cover letter. Do not include any other hospital stays in your answers.

YOUR CARE FROM NURSES

1. **During this hospital stay, how often did nurses treat you with <u>courtesy and respect</u>?**

   ^{1}☐ Never
   ^{2}☐ Sometimes
   ^{3}☐ Usually
   ^{4}☐ Always

2. **During this hospital stay, how often did nurses <u>listen carefully to you</u>?**

   ^{1}☐ Never
   ^{2}☐ Sometimes
   ^{3}☐ Usually
   ^{4}☐ Always

3. **During this hospital stay, how often did nurses <u>explain things</u> in a way you could understand?**

   ^{1}☐ Never
   ^{2}☐ Sometimes
   ^{3}☐ Usually
   ^{4}☐ Always

4. **During this hospital stay, after you pressed the call button, how often did you get help as soon as you wanted it?**

   ^{1}☐ Never
   ^{2}☐ Sometimes
   ^{3}☐ Usually
   ^{4}☐ Always
   ^{9}☐ I never pressed the call button

YOUR CARE FROM DOCTORS

5. During this hospital stay, how often did doctors treat you with <u>courtesy and respect</u>?

   1☐ Never
   2☐ Sometimes
   3☐ Usually
   4☐ Always

6. During this hospital stay, how often did doctors <u>listen carefully to you</u>?

   1☐ Never
   2☐ Sometimes
   3☐ Usually
   4☐ Always

7. During this hospital stay, how often did doctors <u>explain things</u> in a way you could understand?

   1☐ Never
   2☐ Sometimes
   3☐ Usually
   4☐ Always

THE HOSPITAL ENVIRONMENT

8. During this hospital stay, how often were your room and bathroom kept clean?

   1☐ Never
   2☐ Sometimes
   3☐ Usually
   4☐ Always

9. During this hospital stay, how often was the area around your room quiet at night?

   1☐ Never
   2☐ Sometimes
   3☐ Usually
   4☐ Always

YOUR EXPERIENCES IN THIS HOSPITAL

10. During this hospital stay, did you need help from nurses or other hospital staff in getting to the bathroom or in using a bedpan?

    1☐ Yes
    2☐ No → If No, Go to Question 12

11. How often did you get help in getting to the bathroom or in using a bedpan as soon as you wanted?

    1☐ Never
    2☐ Sometimes
    3☐ Usually
    4☐ Always

12. During this hospital stay, did you have any pain?

    1☐ Yes
    2☐ No → If No, Go to Question 15

13. During this hospital stay, how often did hospital staff talk with you about how much pain you had?

    1☐ Never
    2☐ Sometimes
    3☐ Usually
    4☐ Always

14. During this hospital stay, how often did hospital staff talk with you about how to treat your pain?

    1☐ Never
    2☐ Sometimes
    3☐ Usually
    4☐ Always

15. **During this hospital stay, were you given any medicine that you had not taken before?**

    [1] Yes
    [2] No → **If No, Go to Question 18**

16. **Before giving you any new medicine, how often did hospital staff tell you what the medicine was for?**

    [1] Never
    [2] Sometimes
    [3] Usually
    [4] Always

17. **Before giving you any new medicine, how often did hospital staff describe possible side effects in a way you could understand?**

    [1] Never
    [2] Sometimes
    [3] Usually
    [4] Always

WHEN YOU LEFT THE HOSPITAL

18. **After you left the hospital, did you go directly to your own home, to someone else's home, or to another health facility?**

    [1] Own home
    [2] Someone else's home
    [3] Another health facility → **If Another, Go to Question 21**

19. **During this hospital stay, did doctors, nurses or other hospital staff talk with you about whether you would have the help you needed when you left the hospital?**

    [1] Yes
    [2] No

20. **During this hospital stay, did you get information in writing about what symptoms or health problems to look out for after you left the hospital?**

    [1] Yes
    [2] No

OVERALL RATING OF HOSPITAL

Please answer the following questions about your stay at the hospital named on the cover letter. Do not include any other hospital stays in your answers.

21. **Using any number from 0 to 10, where 0 is the worst hospital possible and 10 is the best hospital possible, what number would you use to rate this hospital during your stay?**

    [0] 0   Worst hospital possible
    [1] 1
    [2] 2
    [3] 3
    [4] 4
    [5] 5
    [6] 6
    [7] 7
    [8] 8
    [9] 9
    [10] 10   Best hospital possible

22. **Would you recommend this hospital to your friends and family?**
    1 ☐ Definitely no
    2 ☐ Probably no
    3 ☐ Probably yes
    4 ☐ Definitely yes

UNDERSTANDING YOUR CARE WHEN YOU LEFT THE HOSPITAL

23. **During this hospital stay, staff took my preferences and those of my family or caregiver into account in deciding what my health care needs would be when I left.**
    1 ☐ Strongly disagree
    2 ☐ Disagree
    3 ☐ Agree
    4 ☐ Strongly agree

24. **When I left the hospital, I had a good understanding of the things I was responsible for in managing my health.**
    1 ☐ Strongly disagree
    2 ☐ Disagree
    3 ☐ Agree
    4 ☐ Strongly agree

25. **When I left the hospital, I clearly understood the purpose for taking each of my medications.**
    1 ☐ Strongly disagree
    2 ☐ Disagree
    3 ☐ Agree
    4 ☐ Strongly agree
    5 ☐ I was not given any medication when I left the hospital

ABOUT YOU

There are only a few remaining items left.

26. **During this hospital stay, were you admitted to this hospital through the Emergency Room?**
    1 ☐ Yes
    2 ☐ No

27. **In general, how would you rate your overall health?**
    1 ☐ Excellent
    2 ☐ Very good
    3 ☐ Good
    4 ☐ Fair
    5 ☐ Poor

28. **In general, how would you rate your overall mental or emotional health?**
    1 ☐ Excellent
    2 ☐ Very good
    3 ☐ Good
    4 ☐ Fair
    5 ☐ Poor

29. **What is the highest grade or level of school that you have completed?**
    1 ☐ 8th grade or less
    2 ☐ Some high school, but did not graduate
    3 ☐ High school graduate or GED
    4 ☐ Some college or 2-year degree
    5 ☐ 4-year college graduate
    6 ☐ More than 4-year college degree

30. Are you of Spanish, Hispanic or Latino origin or descent?

¹☐ No, not Spanish/Hispanic/Latino
²☐ Yes, Puerto Rican
³☐ Yes, Mexican, Mexican American, Chicano
⁴☐ Yes, Cuban
⁵☐ Yes, other Spanish/Hispanic/Latino

31. What is your race? Please choose one or more.

¹☐ White
²☐ Black or African American
³☐ Asian
⁴☐ Native Hawaiian or other Pacific Islander
⁵☐ American Indian or Alaska Native

32. What language do you <u>mainly</u> speak at home?

¹☐ English
²☐ Spanish
³☐ Chinese
⁴☐ Russian
⁵☐ Vietnamese
⁶☐ Portuguese
⁹☐ Some other language (please print):
_____

THANK YOU

Please return the completed survey in the postage-paid envelope.

[NAME OF SURVEY VENDOR OR SELF-ADMINISTERING HOSPITAL]

[RETURN ADDRESS OF SURVEY VENDOR OR SELF-ADMINISTERING HOSPITAL]

APPENDIX C

Employee Engagement Survey Sample

NOTE: The results represented below are the average of favorable responses from employees that were connected to the referenced department at the point they were invited to complete the Employee & Provider Engagement Survey.

	Dept	%	Diff
Sustainable Engagement	**76**	**73**	**3**
I am proud to work for or be affiliated with this organization.	100	87	13
There are no substantial obstacles at work to doing my job well.	44	53	-9
I have a good understanding of how my job contributes to this organization achieving its mission, vision and strategic plan.	100	91	9
I am able to sustain the level of energy I need throughout the work day.	75	72	3
This organization provides the resources necessary for me to work effectively (hardware, software, tools, equipment, supplies, etc.).	69	63	6
My work group operates effectively as a team.	88	80	8
The stress levels at work are usually manageable.	50	61	-11
I would recommend this organization to others as a good place to work.	81	74	7
Commitment	**89**	**76**	**13**
I am proud to work for or be affiliated with this organization.	100	87	13
I would prefer to remain with this organization even if a comparable job were available in another organization.	88	73	15
I would recommend this organization to others as a good place to work.	81	74	7
Overall, how satisfied are you with this organization at the present time?	88	70	18
Leadership	**85**	**72**	**13**
I understand the value a large, integrated health system offers our patients and their families.	100	94	6
I have trust and confidence in the work being done by the Senior Leadership of this organization.	69	63	6
This organization has done a good job of clearly describing the work behaviors that demonstrate our mission, vision and strategic plan.	100	80	20
Senior Leadership is accessible and visible to employees.	69	57	12
I trust Senior Leadership to make decisions that are in the best interest of patients and the communities we serve.	88	67	21
Line of Sight	**89**	**82**	**7**
I have a good understanding of how my job contributes to this organization achieving its mission, vision and strategic plan.	100	91	9
I have a good understanding of this organization's mission, vision and strategic plan.	88	87	1
I have a good understanding of the steps we are taking to reach this organization's mission, vision and strategic plan.	81	76	5
This organization does a good job providing information on how well it is performing against its mission, vision and strategic plan.	88	75	13

	Dept	%	Diff
Teamwork	**72**	**68**	**4**
My work group operates effectively as a team.	88	80	8
In this organization, there is generally good teamwork between departments.	75	65	10
There is effective sharing of information across functions.	63	59	4
My work group gets the cooperation it needs from other work groups to achieve our work objectives.	63	69	-6
Well-Being	**79**	**75**	**4**
I am able to sustain the level of energy I need throughout the work day.	75	72	3
My work gives me a sense of personal accomplishment.	88	87	1
The stress levels at work are usually manageable.	50	61	-11
I feel valued as an individual in this organization.	81	62	19
I personally contribute to this organization's success.	100	94	6
Work Environment	**66**	**64**	**2**
There are no substantial obstacles at work to doing my job well.	44	53	-9
This organization provides the resources necessary for me to work effectively (hardware, software, tools, equipment, supplies, etc.).	69	63	0
This organization does a good job of retaining highly qualified employees.	63	57	6
This organization makes patient/customer satisfaction a top priority.	88	82	6

Glossary

A

Adam's Equity Theory (1965). Equity theory is based on perceptions among individual workings comparing one's input–outcome ratio with the input–outcome of another. When the two ratios are equal, equity exists. Inputs are contributions people feel they are making to their environment. For example, one's hard work, loyalty to an organization, amount of time with the organization, as well as individual level of education, training, and skills may become relevant inputs. Outcomes are perceived as rewards someone can receive. Notably, equity perceptions develop as the result of a subjective process as different people may look at similar situations and perceive different levels of equity.

Affective organizational commitment. The emotional attachment, identification, and involvement that an individual has to his or her organization.

Alderfer's ERG Theory (1969). Alderfer's ERG (existence, relatedness and growth) theory is a modification of Maslow's hierarchy of needs. Alderfer presented an empirical test that would lead to the newer ERG theory of human needs. Instead of the five hierarchical needs in Maslow's model, Alderfer proposed that basic human needs may be grouped under three categories: existence, relatedness, and growth. Existence corresponds to Maslow's physiological and safety needs; relatedness corresponds to social needs; and growth refers to Maslow's esteem and self-actualization. ERG theory does not rank needs in any particular order and recognizes that more than one need may operate at a given time. Interestingly, the theory has a "frustration-regression" hypothesis suggesting that individuals who are frustrated in their attempts to satisfy one need may regress to another. Thus, someone who is frustrated by the growth opportunities in his job and progress toward career goals may regress to relatedness need and start spending more time engaging in lesser productive activities, such as social loafing.

Attribution. The behavioral action of regarding something being caused by a person, thing or both.

Attribution Theory. A theory where one seeks to understand the behavior of another by attributing feelings, beliefs, and intentions to them.

Authentic behaviors. Behaviors regarded as courageous, vulnerable, imperfect, introspective, kind, listening, and open-minded.

B

Bedside care employees. Employees directly involved in the care and direct interactions with the patient through the course of the delivery of care.

C

Call button help as soon as wanted. The frequency in which patients received help as soon as desired when nursing was notified via call button.

Causal attribution. The process of trying to determine the cause of individual behavior.

Centers for Medicare and Medicaid (CMS). The Centers for Medicare and Medicaid Services (CMS) operates as the federal agency providing health care coverage through programs associated with Medicaid and Medicare, while also administering the HCAHPS survey measuring patient experience feedback.

Communication with nurses domain. The frequency, and roll-up domain, in which communications with nursing is deemed present in courtesy and respect, nursing listening to patient needs, nursing explaining information in an understandable manner, and the frequency in which patients received help as soon as desired when notified via call button.

Continuance organizational commitment. Commitment to an organization based on personal sacrifice and the necessity to remain employed because of limitations in available options.

Corporate culture. Beliefs and behaviors determining how an organization's employees and management interact both internally and externally. Corporate culture develops organically over time from internal inputs and external influence.

Counterculture. Behaviors and attitudes opposed to, or at variance with, prevailing social and organizational culture norms and objectives.

Certificate of Public Need (COPN). Legislature requiring health care providers wishing to open or expand health care facilities to prove to a regulatory body that their community needs the services the facility would provide. COPN includes the review of existing services and facilities available for the same population.

Critical access hospitals. Rural hospitals providing essential services to rural communities.

Cultural depth and presence. The level of presence of culturally related employee behaviors as measured through bedside care employees.

E

Employee perceptions. Employee perceptions are based on perceived level of cultural factors in the organizational environment measured through bedside employee cultural richness surveys.

Extrinsic motivation factors. Factors related to pay, working conditions, and supervisors; behavior is driven by employees' desire to gain recognition or reward or to avoid punishment or negative judgment.

H

HCAHPS discharge date. The collection of patient experience feedback from the HCAHPS survey based upon the discharge date of the survey. Example:

January "discharge date HCAHPS results" would only reflect the feedback from the patients in the hospital between January 1 and 31.

HCAHPS received date. The collection of patient experience feedback data for a window of time for which the response was received. For example, surveys may be collected in excess of 90 days. A January report of received patient experience data may contain responses from the prior months of September, October, November, and December.

Health Care Consumer Assessment of Health Care Providers and Systems (HCAHPS). The HCAHPS survey is a standardized survey instrument and data collection method utilized to measure patient perspectives on hospital care received.

Herzberg's Motivation Theory (1959). The observation of identifying what satisfies and dissatisfies employees in their job. Herzberg labeled factors causing dissatisfaction as "hygiene" factors because these factors were part of the context in which work is performed, as opposed to the job itself. Hygiene factors include company policies, supervision, working conditions, salary, safety, and job security. In contrast, motivators are factors that are intrinsic to the job, including achievement, recognition, meaningful work, increased responsibilities, advancement, and growth opportunities. According to Herzberg's, motivators are conditions truly encouraging employees to exert greater levels of energy in performance.

Hospital rating. The rating a patient provides on a health care facility based on experiences associated with the delivery of care.

Houston's Public Service Motivation Theory (2008) (Pakdel 2013). Public Service Motivation (PSM) Theory described an approach to motivating employees by investigating motivational behaviors of public sector employees. Public service motivation theory assumes that employees have an ethical motivation to serve the public due to a commitment to the common good, rather than self-interest. The public service motivation approach has significant implications for job choice, performance, and organization effectiveness. Motivation is a measure of participation among public service employees' volunteerism and charity behaviors.

K

Katz Organizational Commitment (1951). Where organizational commitment was described as how workers enter and withdraw from workgroups due to their ability to make decisions within workgroups.

M

Maslow Hierarchy of Needs (1943). Maslow's hierarchy of needs is a popular motivation model and commonly studied among business students and managers. Maslow's theory is based on a simple premise: Human beings have needs that are hierarchically ranked. There are, essentially, needs that are basic to all human beings, and when absent, nothing else matters. As basic needs are satisfied, individuals start looking to satisfy higher order needs. Essentially, once a lower level need is satisfied, it no longer serves as a motivator.

McClelland Acquired Needs Theory (1992). A needs theory positing individuals acquire three types of needs as a result of their life experiences: achievement, affiliation, and power. While all individuals possess some sort of combination of these needs, the dominating need drives employee behavior.

N

Normative organizational commitment. Normative organizational commitment depends on the employee's sense of loyalty, obligation, and comment to membership that provides valuable benefits from belonging to, or being a part of, an organization

Nurses explained things in a way you could understand. The frequency in which nursing explained information to patients in an understandable manner.

Nurses listen carefully to you. The frequency in which nursing carefully listened to patient needs and concerns.

Nurses treated you with courtesy and respect. The frequency in which patients feel they were treated with courtesy and respect.

O

Operational culture. The aspects of the organizational culture that influence outcomes associated with employee performance, driven by behavioral components of organizational culture. Organizational and individual actions inversely influence the culture of the organization.

Organizational commitment. Attachment to, identification with, and involvement of an employee with an organization.

Organizational culture. Organizational culture is the special collection of shared norms and values by individuals and groups in the organization that control the way interactions occur (Moss et al. 2017).

P

Pakdel's Four-Factor Approach to Motivation (2013) (Agarwal and Sajid 2017). Motivation is defined as a phenomenon that is affected by four factors: situation, temperament, goal, and tool. Goals, necessities, and instincts motivate individuals. Aspects of the motivation behavior include behavioral justification, purposefulness, and incidence; the level of energy is different than during previous similar experiences. Five key descriptors of motivation include: (a) motivation factors compel individuals to carry out specific actions; (b) motivation is a behavior that creates energy; (c) motivation begins with a requirement or a deficiency that causes an activation of behavior; (d) motivation is a set of processes that stimulate behavior to achieve goals; and (e) motivation depends on interests.

Patient-centered care. Patient-centered care is an evidence-based concept for improving clinical outcomes and patient satisfaction based on information sharing and availability, including the patient in the diagnosis options regarding decisions and treatment of care, and promoting strong doctor–patient relationships.

Patient experience. Patient experience is based on both the patient perception of quality of care received and the care experience in the delivery of care. Patient experience further encompasses patient perceptions during receipt of care from health care employees and the hospital environment.

Patient liaison groups. Patient liaison groups is a patient-centered care practice based on patient advocacy and services driving patient empowerment with the goal of ensuring that patient and family voices are heard and used to develop and improve outcomes.

Patient perceptions. Patient perceptions are based on the measurable HCAHPS survey questions associated with employee behavior and culture factors. Patient experience is also defined by the influence and drive of perceptions of care based on both compassionate practices and quality of care received.

Personal attribution. The basis of Attribution Theory is that individuals attempt to determine why people behave in particular ways based on a three-stage process: (1) the individual has to observe and perceive the behavior, (2) the individual has to believe the behavior observed was intentionally performed, and (3) the individual must determine if the behavior observed was forced (situational attribution) or not (personal attribution).

R

Responsiveness of hospital staff domain. The frequency, and domain roll-up, in which hospital staff responded to patient needs in time notifying nursing for assistance via nursing call buttons, if patients used the call button, if toileting support was needed, and if toileting support was received as soon as desired.

S

Service workers in a health care environment. In the context of the service worker study, service workers in a health care environment refers to employees serving in a health care facility cleaning and processing linen and laundry items, distributing linen and laundry items, as well as employees services in housekeeping and facility cleaning positions. Service workers in a health care environment in this study exclude administrative and management positions.

Situational attribution. The basis of Attribution Theory is that individuals attempt to determine why people behave in particular ways based on a three-stage process: (1) the individual has to observe and perceive the behavior, (2) the individual has to believe the behavior observed was intentionally performed, and (3) the individual must determine if the behavior observed was forced (situational attribution) or not (personal attribution).

Stay intention. The intention of an employee to remain with his or her organization based on the level of commitment with the organization.

Subculture dependency. The extent to which an organization depends on subculture presence to support organizational needs, goals, and objectives.

Subculture. A culturally connected group operating within a larger culture with shared beliefs, interests, attitudes and values on a more isolated level that may, or may not, be consistent with the larger culture. The subculture group is derived from another culture; typically overall organizational culture in workplace settings.

T

Top Box. Top Box scores are those identified in the instrumentation and data based on the top-level responses to each patient experience survey question. In HCAHPS, this equates to the *Always* measure in terms of frequency and in the 9–10 rating of hospitals by patients.

V

Vroom's Expectancy Theory (1964). Expectancy theory posits the motivation of an individual to put forth more or less effort which is determined by a rational calculation in which individuals evaluate their situation. Expectancy theory holds the view that individuals ask themselves three questions. The first is whether the person believes that high levels of effort will lead to outcomes of interest, such as performance or success. This perception is labeled as *expectancy*. If you believe that the effort you put forth is related to performing well with an attached reward, you are more likely to put forth effort. The second is based on the degree to which the person believes that performance is related to subsequent outcomes, including incentives and rewards. This perception is labeled *instrumentality*. The third theory holds that individuals are concerned about the value of rewards awaiting them as a result of their performance. Anticipated satisfaction that will result from an outcome is referred to as *valence*.

W

Willis Towers Watson. Global advisory and solutions company serving clients to improve internal risk, employee engagement, and workforce analytics.

Bibliography

Acharya, R., and A.K. Dasbiwas. 2018. "A Study on the Relationship between Organizational Commitment and Leadership Style on Paramedical Personnel in Kolkata." *UBIT* 11, no. 1, pp. 80–84.

Adair, J. 2011. *The John Adair Lexicon of Leadership: The Definitive Guide to Leadership Skills and Knowledge.* London: Kogan Page.

Agarwal, P., and S.M. Sajid. 2017. "A Study of Job Satisfaction, Organizational Commitment and Turnover Intention among Public and Private Sector Employees." *Journal of Management Research* 17, no. 3, pp. 123–36.

Ahluwalia, A.K., and K. Preet. 2017. "The Influence of Organizational Commitment on Work Motivation: A Comparative Study of State and Private University Teachers." *The IUP Journal of Organizational Behavior* 16, no. 2, pp. 55-69.

Aksoy, C., H.I. Sengun, and Y. Yilmaz. 2018. "Examination of the Relationship between Job Satisfaction Levels and Organizational Commitments of Tourism Sector Employees: A Research in the Southeastern Anatolia Region of Turkey." *Electronic Journal of Social Sciences* 17, no. 65, pp. 356–5. doi:10.17755/esosder.343032.

Allen, J. 2017. "The Nine Things That Motivate Doctors." *The Hospital Medical Director*, https://hospitalmedicaldirector.com/the-nine-things-that-motivate-doctors/, (accessed July 1, 2019).

American Hospital Association. 2019. "Fast Facts on U.S. Hospitals, 2019." https://www.aha.org/statistics/fast-facts-us-hospitals, (accessed July 1, 2019).

Anders, C., and A. Cassidy. 2014. "Effective Organizational Change in Healthcare: Exploring the Contribution of Empowered Users and Workers." *International Journal of Healthcare Management* 7, no. 2, pp. 132–51. doi:10.1179/2047971913Y.000000061.

Andre, B., E. Sjovold, T. Rannestad, and G.I. Ringdal. 2013. "The Impact of Work Culture on Quality of Care in Nursing Homes – A Review Study." *Scandinavian Journal of Caring Sciences* 3, pp. 449–57. doi:10.1111/scs.12086.

Antoni, C., Baeten, X., S. Perkins, J. Shaw, and M. Vartiainen. 2017. "Linking Employee Motivation and Organizational Performance." *Journal of Personnel Psychology* 16, no. 2, pp. 57–60. doi:10.1027/1866-5888/a000187.

Anvari, R., Z. JianFu, and H. Chermahini. 2014. "Effective Strategy for Solving Voluntary Turnover Problem Among Employees." *Social and Behavioral Sciences* 129, pp. 186–90. doi:10.1016/j.sbspro.2014.03.665.

Baba, M.M. 2017. "Emotional Intelligence, Organization Commitment, and Job Satisfaction: A Study of Higher Learning Institutions." *Amity Global Business Review* 12, no. 2, pp. 51–60.

Bala, P. 2016. "Is the Talent War Worth Fighting?" *Campaign Asia-Pacific*, p. 50.

Bassett-Jones, N., and G.C. Lloyd. 2005. "Does Herzberg's Motivation Theory Have Staying Power?" *The Journal of Management Development* 24, no. 10, pp. 929–43.

Bauer, T., and B. Erdogan. 2015. *Organizational Behavior*. Boston: Flatworld.

Bavik, A. 2016. "Developing a New Hospitality Industry Organizational Culture Scale." *International Journal of Hospitality Management* 58, pp. 44–55. doi:10.1016/j.ijhm.2016.07.005.

Bellou, V. 2008. "Identifying Organizational Culture and Subcultures within Greek Public Hospitals." *Journal of Health, Organization and Management* 22, no. 5, pp. 495–509. doi:10.1108/14777290910898714.

Birkelien, N.L. 2017. "A Strategic Framework for Improving the Patient Experience in Hospitals." *Journal of Healthcare Management* 62, no. 4, pp. 251–9. doi:10.1097/JHM-D-17-00071.

Blau, P.M. 1964. *Exchange and Power in Social Life*. New York: Wiley.

Brunoro-Kadash, C., and N. Kadash. 2013. "Time to Care: A Patient-Centered Quality Improvement Strategy." *Leadership in Health Services* 25, no. 3, pp. 220–31.

Bryant, S. 2013. "Organizational Culture of Mississippi Hospitals as Perceived by Laboratory Professionals." *Clinical Laboratory Science* 26, no. 3, pp. 147–52.

Bureau of Labor Statistics. n.d.-a. "Employment and Unemployment Summary." https://www.bls.gov/news.release/laus.nr0.htm, (accessed April 7, 2019).

Bureau of Labor Statistics. n.d.-b. "Employment Situation Summary." https://www.bls.gov/news.release/empsit.nr0.htm, (accessed April 7, 2019).

Carter, J.C. and F.N. Silverman. 2016. "Using HCAHPS Data to Improve Hospital Care Quality." *Total Quality Management Journal* 28, no. 6, pp. 974–90, doi:10.1108/TQM-09-2014-0072.

Celis, N.J. 2018. "Compliance Theory: A Case Study Approach in Understanding Organizational Commitment." *DLSU Business and Economics Review* 27, no. 2, pp. 88–118.

Centers for Medicare and Medicaid Services. 2018. "The HCAHPS Survey—Frequently Asked Questions." https://www.cms.gov/medicare/quality-initiatives-patient-assessment-instruments/hospitalqualityinits/downloads/hospitalhcahpsfactsheet201007.pdf, (accessed March 25, 2019).

Cesario, F., and M.J. Chambel. 2017. "Linking Organizational Commitment and Work Engagement to Employee Performance." *Knowledge and Process Management* 24, no. 2, pp. 152–8. doi:10.1002/kpm.1542.

Chen, C.A., D.Y. Chen, and C. Xu. 2018. "Applying Self-Determination Theory to Understand Public Employees' Motivation for a Public Service Career: An

East Asian Case (Taiwan)." *Public Performance and Management Review* 41, no. 2, pp. 365–89. doi:10.1080/15309576.2018.1431135.

Chen, J.I., G.D. Romero, and M.S. Karver. 2016. "The Relationship of Perceived Campus Culture to Mental Health Help-Seeking Intentions." *Journal of Counseling Psychology*, 63, no. 6, pp. 677–84. doi:10.1027/cou0000095.

Choi, C.J., S.W. Hwang, and H.N. Kim. 2015. "Changes in the Degree of Patient Expectations for Patient-Centered Care in a Primary Care Setting." *Korean Journal of Family Medicine* 36, no. 2, pp. 103–12. doi:10.1042/KJFM.2015.36.2.103.

Christiansen, N., M. Sliter, and C.T. Frost. 2014. "What Employees Dislike About Their Jobs: Relationship Between Personality-Based Fit and Work Satisfaction." *Personality and Individual Differences* 71, pp. 25–29. doi:10.1016/j.paid.2014.07.013.

Cosgrove, D.M., M. Fisher, P. Gabow, G.C. Halvorson, B.C. James, G.S. Kaplan, G.S. Perline, R. Petzel, G.D. Steele, and J.S. Toussaint. 2013. "Ten Strategies to Lower Costs, Improve Quality, and Engage Patients: The View from Leading Health System CEOs." *Health Affairs* 32, no. 2, pp. 321–7. doi:10.1377/hlthaff.2012.1074.

Costello, R., and S.A. Welch. 2014. "A Qualitative Analysis of Faculty and Study Perceptions of Effective Online Class Communities Using Herzberg's Motivator-Hygiene Factors." *The Quarterly Review of Distance Education* 15, no. 4, pp. 15-23.

Daft, R.L. 2007. *Organizational Theory and Design* (9th ed.). Mason: Thomson.

Daw, D., and P.E. Khoury. 2014. "Herzberg's Motivation-Hygiene Theory and Job Dissatisfaction in the Lebanese Banking Sector." *Business Journal for Entrepreneurs* 2014, no. 3, pp. 68–82.

Denison, D.R. and A.K. Mishra. 1995. "Toward a Theory of Organizational Culture and Effectiveness." *Organizational Science* 6, no. 2, pp. 204–23.

Dinc, M.S. 2017. "Organizational Commitment Components and Performance: Mediating Role of Job Satisfaction." *Pakistan Journal of Commerce and Social Sciences* 11, no. 3, pp. 773–89.

Doyle, A. 2016. "Beebe Healthcare's Compassion Recognition Program Empowers Staff to Connect with Patients, their Families and One Another." *Industry Edge*, http://www.pressganey.com/docs/default-source/industry-edge/issue-10---november/beebe-healthcare-39-s-compassion-recognition-program-empowers-staff-to-connect-with-patients-their-families-and-one-another.pdf, (accessed July 25, 2019).

Dunn, K. 2016. "Who to Hire When Your Culture Sucks." *Workforce* 95, no. 7, p. 13.

Dzaher, A. 2017. "4 Key Factors That Motivate Nurses in Their Career." *MIMS Today*, https://today.mims.com/4-key-factors-that-motivate-nurses-in-their-career, (accessed July 25, 2019).

Elzweig, M. 2017. "Recruiting wars." *Career*, pp. 27–28.

Fareed, K.A., and F.A. Jan. 2016. "Cross-Cultural Validation Test of Herzberg's Two-Factor Theory: An Analysis of Bank Officers Working in Khyber Pakhtunkhwa." *Journal of Managerial Sciences* 10, no. 2, pp. 285–300.

Gagne, M. and E.L. Deci. 2005. "Self-Determination Theory and Work Motivation." *Journal of Organizational Behavior* 26, no. 4, pp. 331–62.

Gutierrez, A.P., L.L. Candela, and L. Carver. 2012. "The Structural Relationship Between Organizational Commitment, Global Job Satisfaction, Developmental Experiences, Work Values, Organizational Support, and Person-Organization Fit Among Nursing Faculty." *Journal of Advanced Nursing* 68, no. 7, pp. 1601–14. doi:10.1111/j.1365-2648.2012.05990.x.

Hahtela, N., B. McCormak, D. Doran, E. Paavilainen, P. Slater, M. Helminen, and T. Suominen. 2017. "Workplace Culture and Patient Outcomes: What's the Connection?" *Nursing Management* 48, no. 12, pp. 35–44. doi:10.1097/01.NUMA.0000526910.24168.

Hart, T.A., J.B. Gilstrap, and M.C. Bolino. 2016. "Organizational Citizenship Behavior and the Enhancement of Absorptive Capacity." *Journal of Business Research* 69, no. 10, pp. 3981–3988. doi:10.1016/j.jbusres.2016.06.001.

Hayes, A.F., and N.J. Rockwood. 2017. "Regression-Based Statistical Mediation and Moderation Analysis in Clinical Research: Observations, Recommendations, and Implementation." *Behavior Research and Therapy* 98, pp. 39–57. doi:10.1016/j.brat.2016.11.001.

HCAHPS Online. n.d. "Hospital Consumer Assessment of Healthcare Providers and Systems." http://www.hcahpsonline.org/en/survey-instruments/, (accessed July 1, 2019).

Heidenreich, P. 2013. "Time for a Thorough Evaluation of Patient Centered Care." *Circulation: Cardiovascular Quality and Outcomes* 6, pp. 2–4. doi:10.1161/circoutcomes.112.970194.

Hunt, S.R., J.C. Probst, K.S. Haddock, R. Moran, S.L. Baker, R.A. Anderson, and K. Corazzini. 2012. "Registered Nurse Retention Strategies in Nursing Homes: A Two-Factor Perspective." *Healthcare Management Review* 37, no. 3, pp. 246–56. doi:10.1097/HMR.0b013e3182352425.

Iannuzzi, J.C., S.A. Kahn, L. Zhang, M.L. Gestring, K. Noyes, and J.R. Monson. 2015. "Getting Satisfaction: Drivers of Surgical Hospital Consumer Assessment of Health Care Providers and Systems Survey Scores." *Journal of Surgical Research* 197, pp. 155–61. doi:10.1016/j.jss.2015.03.045.

International Council on Active Aging. 2018. "81% of Employers Aspire to a Culture of Wellbeing." *International Council on Active Aging* 18, no. 24.

Jacobs, R., R. Mannion, H.T. Davies, S. Harrison, F. Konteh, and K. Walshe. 2013. "The Relationship Between Organizational Culture and Performance in Acute Care Hospitals." *Social Science and Medicine* 76, pp. 115–125. doi:10.1016/j.socsimed.2012.10.014.

Jena, L.K., P. Bhattacharyya, and S. Pradhan. 2017. "Employee Engagement and Affective Organizational Commitment: Mediating Role of Employee Voice Among Indian Service Sector Employees." *Vision* 21, no. 4, pp. 356–66. doi:10.1177/0972262917733170.

Johnson, H. 2019a. "The Influence of Workplace Motivation Factors on Organizational Commitment Among Healthcare Service Workers." Doctoral dissertation, South University.

Johnson, H. 2019b. *Motivational Equilibrium.* Bradenton: BookLocker.

Kahn, R.L., and A.S. Tannenbaum. 1957. "Leadership Practices and Member Participation in Local Unions." *Personnel Psychology* 10, pp. 277–92.

Karami, A., J. Farokhzadian, and G. Foroughameri. 2017. "Nurses' Professional Competency and Organizational Commitment: Is it Important for Human Resource Management?" *PloS One* 12, no. 11, pp. 1–15. doi:10.1371/journal.pone.0187863.

Katenova, M., M. Mahmood, and M. Sharfaraj. 2016. "Job Satisfaction in a Transition Economy: Is Herzberg's Theory Valid in Kazakhstan?" *Journal of International Management Studies* 13, no. 2, pp. 61–66.

Katz, D. 1951. *Survey Research Center: An Overview of the Human Relations Program, Groups, Leadership, and Men.* Pittsburgh: Carnegie Press.

Khera, A. 2017. "Impact of Organizational Commitment on Burnout: A Study Among the Employees in a Retail Sector in India." *International Journal of Research in Commerce and Management* 8, no. 7, pp. 58–62.

Kleefstra, S.M., L.C. Zandbelt, H.J. deHaes, and R.B. Kool. 2015. "Trends in Patient Satisfaction in Dutch University Medical Centers: Room for Improvement for All." *BMC Health Services Research* 15, no. 112, pp. 1–9. doi:10.1186/s12913-015-0766-7.

Kotni, V.V.D.P., and V. Karumuri. 2018. "Application of Herzberg's Two-Factor Theory Model for Motivating Retail Salesforces." *The IUP Journal of Organizational Behavior,* 16, no. 1, pp. 24–42.

LaFerney, M. 2018. "Point of Care: What Motivates You as a Nurse?" *Reflections on Nursing Leadership,* https://www.reflectionsonnursingleadership.org/features/more-features/point-of-care-what-motivates-you-as-a-nurse, (accessed July 20, 2019).

Lapointe, E., and C. Vandenberghe. 2018. "Examination of the Relationships Between Servant Leadership, Organizational Commitment, and Voice and Antisocial Behaviors." *Journal of Business Ethics* 148, pp. 99–115. doi:10.1007/s10551-015-3002-9.

Lateef, F. 2017. "When it Comes to Debriefing, Does Culture Eat Strategy?" *Education in Medicine Journal* 9, no. 2, pp. 69–74. doi:10.21315/eimg2017.9.2.9.

Lavoie-Tremblay, M., P. O'Connor, A. Biron, B. McGibbon, G. Cyr, and J. Frechette. 2016. "The Experience of Patients Engaged in Co-Designing

Care Processes." *The Health Care Manager* 35, no. 4, pp. 284–93. doi:10.1097/HCM0000000000000132.

Lazaroiu, G. 2015. "Work Motivation and Organizational Behavior." *Contemporary Readings in Law and Social Justice* 7, no. 2, pp. 66–75.

Leroy, H., and M.E. Palanski. 2012. "Authentic Leadership and Behavioral Integrity as Drivers of Follower Commitment and Performance." *Journal of Business Ethics* 107, pp. 255–64. doi:10.1007/s10551-011-1036-1.

Li, X., J. Zhang, S. Zhang, and M. Zhou. 2017. "A Multilevel Analysis of the Role of Interactional Justice in Promoting Knowledge-Sharing Behavior: The Mediated Role of Organizational Commitment." *Industrial Marketing Management* 62, pp. 226–33 doi:10.1016/jindmarman.2016.09.006.

Lizote, S.A., M.A. Verdinelli, and S. Nascimento. 2017. "Organizational Commitment and Job Satisfaction: A Study with Municipal Civil Servants." *Brazilian Journal of Public Administration*, no. 6, pp. 947–67. doi:10.1590/00347612156382.

Lok, P., and J. Crawford. 2017. "The Relationship Between Commitment and Organizational Culture, Subculture, Leadership Style, and Job Satisfaction in Organizational Change and Development." *Leadership and Organization Development Journal* 20, no. 7, pp. 365–73.

Lundberg, C., A. Gudmundson, and T.D. Andersson. 2009. "Herzberg's Two-Factor Theory of Work Motivation Tested Empirically on Seasonal Workers in Hospitality and Tourism." *Tourism Management* 30, pp. 890–99. doi:10.1016/j.tour.man.2008.12.003.

Luo, N., X. Guo, B. Lu, and G. Chen. 2018. "Can Non-Work-Related Social Media Use Benefit the Company? A Study on Corporate Blogging and Affective Organizational Commitment." *Computers in Human Behavior* 81, pp. 84–92. doi:10.1016/j.chb.2017.12.004.

Mallidou, A.A., G.G. Cummings, C.A. Estabrooks, and P.B. Giovannetti. 2010. "Nurse Specialty Subcultures and Patient Outcomes in Acute Care Hospitals: A Multiple-Group Structural Equation Modeling." *International Journal of Nursing Studies* 48, 81–93.

Matei, M.C., and M.M. Abrudan. 2016. "Adapting Herzberg's Two-Factor Theory to the Cultural Context of Romania." *Social and Behavioral Sciences* 221, pp. 95–104, doi:10.1016/j.sbspro.2016.05.094.

McClelland, L.E., and T.J. Vogus. 2014. "Compassion Practices and HCAHPS: Does Rewarding and Supporting Workplace Compassion Influence Patient Perceptions?" *Health Services Research* 49, no. 5. doi:10.1111/1475-6773.12186.

McShane, S., and M. Von Glinow. 2009. *Organizational Behavior*. New York: McGraw-Hill.

Merlino, J. n.d. "Teaching Hospitals: Adding Culture to the Curriculum." *Industry Edge*, http://www.pressganey.com/resources/articles/teaching-hospitals-adding-culture-to-the-curriculum, (accessed July 30, 2019).

Minority Nurse. 2015. "Nursing Statistics," https://minoritynurse.com/nursing-statistics/, (accessed March 31, 2019).

Moss, S., M. Mitchell, and V. Casey. 2017. "Creating a Culture of Success: Using the Magnet Recognition Program as a Framework to Engage Nurses in an Australian Healthcare Facility." *The Journal of Nursing Administration* 47, no. 2, pp. 116–22, doi:10.1097/NNA.0000000000000450.

Ortega, A.O., J.S. Corona, E.S. Hernandez, O. Montano, J. Garnica, S.A. Garduno, and C. Robles. 2015. "A Systematic Model of Analysis of Organizational Culture in Healthcare Services." *Nova Scientia* 7, no. 15, pp. 321–42.

Ortega-Parra, A., and M.A. Sastre-Castillo. 2013. "Impact of Perceived Corporate Culture on Organizational Commitment." *Management Decision* 51, no. 5, pp. 1071–83. doi:10.1108/MD-08-2012-0599.

Overby, S. 2013. "The Great Talent Hunt." *Leadership*, pp. 32–44.

Ozturk, E.B., G. Karagonlar, and S. Emirza. 2016. "Relationship Between Job Insecurity and Emotional Exhaustion: Moderating Effects of Prevention Focus and Affective Organizational Commitment." *International Journal of Stress Management*, 24, no. 3, pp. 247–69. doi:10.1037/str000037.

Pakdel, B. 2013. "The Historical Context of Motivation and Analysis Theories Individual Motivation." *International Journal of Humanities and Social Science,* 3, no. 18, 240–7.

Paterson, J. 2014. "78% of Global Employers Committed to a Healthy Workplace Culture. *Employee Benefits,* https://employeebenefits.co.uk/78-of-global-employers-committed-to-healthy-workplace-culture/ (accessed 12 December 2019).

Perez-Perez, M., M.J. Vela-Jimenez, S. Abella-Garces, and A. Martinez-Sanchez. 2017. "Work-Family Practices and Organizational Commitment: The Mediator Effect of Job Satisfaction." *Universia Business Review* 56, pp. 52–83. doi:10.3232/UBR.2017.V14.N4.03.

Pilav, A., and Z. Jatic. 2017. "The Impact of Organizational Culture on Patient Satisfaction." *Journal of Health Sciences* 7, no. 1, pp. 9–14.

Potipiroon, W., and M.T. Ford. 2017. "Does Public Service Motivation Always Lead to Organizational Commitment? Examining the Moderating Roles of Intrinsic Motivation and Ethical Leadership." *Public Personnel Management* 46, no. 3, pp. 211–38. doi:10.1177/0091026017717241.

Rafael, G., G. Goncalves, J. Santos, A. Orgambidez-Ramos, and C. Sousa. 2017. "Explanatory Contribution of Social Responsibility and Organizational Justice on Organizational Commitment: An Exploratory Study in a Higher Public Education Institution." *Polish Psychological Bulletin* 48, no. 4, pp. 470–80. doi:10.1515/ppb-2017-0054.

Raso, R. 2013. "Value-Based Purchasing: What's the Real Score? Reward or Penalty, Step up to the Plate." *Nursing Management* 44, no. 5, pp. 29–35.

Ratanawongsa, N., E.E. Howell, and S.M. Wright. 2006. "What Motivations Physicians Throughout Their Careers in Medicine?" *Comprehensive Therapy* 32, no. 4, pp. 210–17.

Reis, G., J. Trullen, and J. Story. 2016. "Perceived Organizational Culture and Engagement: The Meditating Role of Authenticity." *Journal of Managerial Psychology* 31, no. 6, pp. 1091–1106. doi:10.1108/JMP-06-2015-0178.

Richardson, A. 2004. "Creating a Culture of Compassion: Developing Supportive Care for People with Cancer." *European Journal of Oncology Nursing* 8, pp. 293–305.

Robert, G., R. Waite, J. Cornwell, E. Morrow, and J. Maben. 2014. "Understanding and Improving Patient Experience: A National Survey of Training Courses Provided by Higher Education Providers and Healthcare Organizations in England." *Nurse Education Today* 34, pp. 112–20. doi:10.1016/j.nedt.2012.012.

Ryan, C. 2017. "Sustaining and Growing a Winning Culture." *Journal of Healthcare Management* 62, no. 6, pp. 361–65. doi:10.1097/JHM-D-17-00161.

Saillour-Glenisson, F., S. Domecq, M. Kret, M. Sibe, J.P. Dumond, P. Michel, and the OReM Group. 2016. "Design and Validation of a Questionnaire to Assess Organizational Culture in French Hospital Wards." *BioMed Central Health Services Research* 16, no. 491, pp. 1–14. doi:10.1186/s12913-016-1736-4.

Salkind, N.J. 2010. *Encyclopedia of Research Design.* Thousand Oaks: Sage.

Schein, E.H. 1992. *Organizational Culture and Leadership.* San Francisco, CA: Jossey-Bass.

Schmiedel, T., J Vom Brocke, and J. Recker. 2013. "Development and Validation of an Instrument to Measure Organizational Cultures' Support of Business Process Management." *Journal of Information and Management* 51, pp. 43–56. doi:10.1016/j.im.2013.08.005.

Scott, T., R. Mannion, H. Davis, and M. Marshall. 2003. "The Quantitative Measurement of Organizational Culture in Healthcare: A Review of the Available Instruments." *Health Services Research* 38, no. 3, pp. 923–45. doi:10.1111/1475-6773.00154.

Sharma, D. 2016. "Organizational Commitment and Organizational Effectiveness." *International Journal of Research in Commerce and Management* 7, no. 1, pp. 22–28.

Spanuth, T., and A. Wald. 2017. "Understanding the Antecedents of Organizational Commitment in the Context of Temporary Organizations: An Empirical Study." *Scandinavian Journal of Management* 33, pp. 129–38. doi:10.1016/j.scaman.2017.06.002.

Statista. 2019. "Number of All Hospitals in the U.S. 1975-2017." *Statista,* https://www.statista.com/statistics/185843/number-of-all-hospitals-in-the-us-since-2001/, (accessed April 2, 2019).

Taylor, B. 2015. "The Integrated Dynamics of Motivation and Performance in the Workplace." *Performance Improvement* 54, no. 5, pp. 28-37. doi:10.1002/pfi.21481.

Tosun, N., and H. Ulusoy. 2017. "The Relationship of Organizational Commitment, Job Satisfaction, and Burnout on Physicians and Nurses." *Journal of Economics and Management* 28, no. 2, pp. 90–111. doi:10.22367/jem2017.28.06.

Trenev, V.N. 2018. "Modeling the Successful Development of an Organization based on the Trajectory Approach." *Journal of Entrepreneurship Education* 21, pp. 1–12.

Truxillo, D. 2015. "Commonsense Talent Management: Using Strategic Human Resources to Improve Company Performance." *Personnel Psychology* 68, no. 2, pp. 453–55. doi:10.1111/peps.12102_4.

Turner, A. 2017. "How Does Intrinsic and Extrinsic Motivation Drive Performance Culture in Organizations?" *Cogent Education*, pp. 1-5. doi:10.1080/2331186X.2017.1337543.

Uhl-Bien, M., J.R., Schermerhorn, and R.N. Osborn. 2014. *Organizational Behavior: Experience, Grow, Contribute*. Hoboken, NJ: Wiley.

Valeau, P., J. Wilems, and H. Parak. 2016. "The Effect of Attitudinal and Behavioral Commitment on the Internal Assessment of Organizational Effectiveness: A Multi-Level Analysis." *International Society for Third-Sector Research* 27, pp. 2913–2936. doi:10.1007/s11266-016-9703-6.

Vijayakumar, V.S.R., and U. Saxena. 2015. "Herzberg Revisited: Dimensionality and Structural Invariance of Herzberg's Two-Factor Model." *Journal of the Indian Academy of Applied Psychology* 41, no. 2, pp. 291–98.

Weiner, B. 2019. "Attribution Theory." *Instructional Design*, https://www.instructionaldesign.org/theories/attribution-theory/, (accessed June 15, 2019).

Williams and Glisson. 2014. "Testing a Theory of Organizational Culture, Climate, and Youth Outcomes in Child Welfare Systems: A United States National Study." *Child Abuse and Neglect* 38, pp. 757–767, https://doi.org/10.1016/j.chiabu.2013.09.003.

Wombacher, N.J., and C. Felfe. 2017. "The Interplay of Team and Organizational Commitment in Motivation Employees' Interteam Conflict Handling." *Academy of Management Journal* 60, no. 4, pp. 1554–1581. doi:10.5465/amj.2014.0718.

Wood, R., and A. Bandura. 1989. "Social Cognitive Theory of Organizational Management." *Academy of Management Review* 14, no. 3, pp. 361–84.

Zachariadou, T., S. Zannetos, and A. Pavlakis. 2013. "Organizational Culture in the Primary Healthcare Setting of Cyprus." *BioMed Central Health Services Research* 13, no. 1, pp. 1–8. doi:10.1186/1472-6963-12-112.

About the Author

Dr. Hesston L. Johnson is an expert in the field of leadership and organizational behavior, with more than 15 years of experience in management and leadership. His expertise is in health care operations leadership, leadership development and consulting, workplace motivation, employee commitment, and health care efficiencies consulting. Research by Dr. Johnson includes observational and correlation studies in health care settings focused on bedside care nursing employees and patient experience measures, the correlations between health care support service worker motivation and affective organizational commitment, and frontline service worker motivation factor analyses. He has also completed multiple case studies, including observations in high functioning cultures in health care met with disruption from organizational leadership, as well as organizational behavior measures among highly engaged employees within organizations with significant turnover challenges. He is a member of the American Management Association, Organizational Behavior Management, International Leadership Association, and Delta Mu Delta International Business Society.

Index

OTHER TITLES IN OUR HEALTH CARE MANAGEMENT COLLECTION

David Dilts, Oregon Health & Science University (OHSU)
and Lawrence Fredendall, Clemson University, *Editors*

- *Quality Management in a Lean Health Care Environment* by Daniel Collins
  and Melissa Mannon
- *Improving Healthcare Management at the Top: How Balanced Boardrooms Can Lead to
  Organizational Success* by Milan Frankl and Sharon Roberts
- *The Patient Paradigm Shifts: Profiling the New Healthcare Consumer* by Judy L. Chan
- *Leading Adaptive Teams in Healthcare Organizations*
  by Kurt C. O'Brien and Christopher E. Johnson
- *Management Skills for Clinicians, Volume I: Transitioning to Administration*
  by Linda R. LaGanga
- *Management Skills for Clinicians, Volume II: Advancing Your Skills* by Linda R. LaGanga
- *The DNA of Physician Leadership: Creating Dynamic Executives*
  by Myron J. Beard and Steve Quach
- *Predictive Medicine: Artificial Intelligence and Its Impact on Healthcare Business
  Strategy* by Emmanuel Fombu

Announcing the Business Expert Press Digital Library

Concise e-books business students need for classroom and research

This book can also be purchased in an e-book collection by your library as

- a one-time purchase,
- that is owned forever,
- allows for simultaneous readers,
- has no restrictions on printing, and
- can be downloaded as PDFs from within the library community.

Our digital library collections are a great solution to beat the rising cost of textbooks. E-books can be loaded into their course management systems or onto students' e-book readers.

The **Business Expert Press** digital libraries are very affordable, with no obligation to buy in future years. For more information, please visit **www.businessexpertpress.com/librarians**. To set up a trial in the United States, please email **sales@businessexpertpress.com**.

www.ingramcontent.com/pod-product-compliance
Lightning Source LLC
Chambersburg PA
CBHW061326220326
41599CB00026B/5052